Chinese Playground

A Memoir

Bill Lee

Rhapsody Press • San Francisco

http://www.chineseplayground.com
email: mail@chineseplayground.com
Printed in the United States of America
Second Hardcover Edition: April 1999
Published by:
Rhapsody Press
P.O. Box 27222
San Francisco, CA 94127

For my son, Eric

In memory of Ellen Nash

Acknowledgments

Vivian Young for her cover design and layout of the text; Kathy Glass, for polishing the manuscript; Naomi Wong, for proofreading the draft; and Michael Zimmerman, who was my writing professor at San Francisco State University.

Special thanks to Chun Chiu, George Hwang, Frank Lee and Norm Godihno for guiding me through one of the most intense start-ups in Silicon Valley. I'd like to express my appreciation to the former employees at Sun Microsystems' TOPS division, who went out of their way to make me feel welcome.

My gratitude goes out to Dorothy Lee (unrelated) and Linda Plack at George Washington High School, as well as Jones Wong, Phil Wong, Kan Chin and Joe Sweeney of the San Francisco Police Department, for their concern and assistance with Eric.

I owe my life to physician Dr. Larry Shore and his wonderful staff, and psychotherapist Dr. Andrea Polk. I credit the healing of my spirit and the serenity I've gained to my sponsors and the loving brothers and sisters in my recovery fellowship. You know who you are and how special you are to me.

To my biological sisters Mary, Dorothy, and May—thanks for watching over me as we were growing up. Perhaps this book will help you understand who I am today. I've done my best to guard your secrets.

Second Edition

Leah Garchik for her kindness and support; Kevin Ryan and the staff at Green Apple Books in San Francisco for believing in the story.

CONTENTS

Preface

PART ONE:

1

Chinatown's Dirty Secrets

2

Chinese Playground

3

Keeping Up with the Wongs

4

Hock Sair Woey, The Chinese Underworld

5

Doin' the Nine-Ball Hustle

6

"Riding the Water," Secret Society Executions

7

Joe Boys

8

The Golden Dragon Massacre

PART TWO:

9

A Chinese Soap Opera

10

The *Tao* of Corporate Warfare

11

High-Tech Warrior

12

Massacre in Silicon Valley

Epilogue

PREFACE

Chinese Playground began as an assignment for my psychology class in 1975. Undergraduate students were required to write an autobiography. Before submitting my work, I secured absolute confidentiality from my professor. Needless to say, he was shocked at the contents, which included an exposé on my family as well as the Chinese Underworld.

After the Golden Dragon Massacre in 1977, followed by the subsequent arrests and convictions of my close friends, I was compelled to write my version of the Chinatown gang war under a pseudonym. I soon realized that my identity would be apparent and the risks were too great.

The fact remains that to my knowledge, there has never been a complete literary work presented from inside the Chinese Underworld. Journalists, educators and sociologists have reported on specific crimes, conducted interviews or indirectly recounted experiences from former gang members. Facts were either inaccurate or voices of the characters diminished.

Following the ESL Massacre, I had a riveting story to share regarding the rampage and five-plus hours siege. In compliance with a gag order issued on the case by the presiding judge, I decided to wait until Richard Farley's trial had ended before going public. After Farley was sentenced, I lacked the motivation and discipline to complete the project.

Writing this memoir during my emotional recovery allowed me to express myself honestly and with humility. The process served as a catharsis and was a milestone in my healing. Earlier versions would have been shallow, dark and arrogant.

Although a number of publishers (local and New York-based) expressed interest in the book, I decided to self-publish in order to retain my voice in the narrative. I discovered the literary world to be extremely subjective and the developmental input I received from agents and editors were inconsistent.

This is a true story about destiny, involving my dark journey through life. It is presented simply and straightforwardly. All events in the book occurred. Some names, dates and locations have been altered to protect the identities of victims and those who wish to remain anonymous.

A towering police officer chases after me as I run out of the playground into the alley. Heading north past Uncle's Cafe, I crash into startled shoppers who scream at me in Cantonese. Each time I look, he's gaining ground. As I reach Washington Street and turn left, the rattling of his keys, whistle and handcuffs indicates that he is extremely close. Before I know it, he lunges and grabs hold of my jacket. Instinctively, I extend both arms back, slipping free.

Running into the street, between moving cars as they blast their horns, I reach Ross Alley. "Tiger," a fellow gang member who was murdered a few blocks away, is standing on the corner. He has a large hole in his chest and he's smiling at me. The sun's rays are passing through his fatal gunshot wound. Curious, I stop and put my hand through the opening. It feels like I'm sticking my fingers into a jacuzzi.

"Tiger, are you alright?"

"Hey, William, where's all the guys, man?"

"Everybody got busted for the massacre, Tiger," I reply. "They were getting revenge for you."

"So what happened to you?" he asks.

"Hell, the cops questioned me about the murders and some of the guys thought I was an informant. They almost bumped me off by mistake."

"Oh, I saw your father," Tiger says.

"Is he in heaven or hell?" I ask.

"He went down there," he replies, pointing midway down the alley. "Go on...look for your father. Just be careful."

I slowly enter the alley, which is darkened by shadows. It is deserted except for what appears to be two winos lying on the ground a few feet from one another. Moving closer, I see blood gushing from their bodies. The streams of blood from the men are flowing along the asphalt's cracks and dripping into the gutter between them.

A man stumbles out of a nightclub and falls in front of me, his face slashed from top to bottom. He is bleeding profusely and moaning. Recognizing the victims, I begin retreating backwards.

As I glance at a storefront window, I see a reflection of a little boy, barely four feet tall. It's me—wearing my old favorite Levi's jeans, a hand-me-down plaid shirt and white Converse high-tops.

Approaching the pawn shop where my grandfather worked, I recognize the man inside, through the iron gate. He's fondling the breasts of a half-naked young woman. It's my father when he was younger. His hair is glistening black, like in the earliest photos he took with my mother. Spotting me, he rushes over, holding my chipped rice bowl containing one of his herbal brews. As I'm standing still, unsure of what to make of his appearance and behavior, my father aggressively pushes the potion up against my mouth. The stench is sickening; the look in his eyes, frightening.

"You're trying to poison me!" *I scream.*

"You weren't supposed to be born!" *he shouts.*

I slap the bowl away and take off running. Approaching the far end of the alley, I see a large group of youths blocking the path. Moving closer, I recognize my old blood-brothers as well as rival gang members, standing on opposite sides. They simultaneously draw their guns. Instead of facing off, they all turn and point their weapons at me. Click...click...click. Triggers being pulled are heard.

God, they all want me dead!

With everyone closing in on me, I back up and leap into a doorway. Its brown metal frame with tinted glass stands out among the deteriorating wood of surrounding structures. Above the entrance is the Chinese death number, "four" (saey).

With nowhere else to run, I decide to go in. Only I can't seem to move. I twist and turn, but my legs are restricted.

I wake up and my feet are entangled in the blankets. The room is completely dark and my wife, laying next to me, is snoring like a little mouse. As I sit up on the bed, relieved that it was only a nightmare, my throat feels bone-dry. Longing for a glass of water, I simply flop back down, half-asleep and exhausted.

Entering what appears to be an office building, I see rows of bright fluorescent lights hanging from the ceiling. The first room to my left has a door with wire-meshed glass panes. Looking in, I see the bathroom of my family's Chinatown apartment. On the floor, my mother lies unconscious in a pool of blood. The sink, tub and walls are covered with giant cockroaches, rapidly descending on her.

My child self begins yelling, "Mommy! Mommy!" Desperate to reach her, I try turning the knob on the door. Not only is it locked, it's sizzling hot. The nuns at Saint Mary's warned us that suicide will lead you to hell, I remind myself.

Dashing down the dark, narrow hallway, I peek into a room on the right side. Jack Carson, the chairman of the start-up company I worked at, is screaming at his executive staff in a smoke-filled conference room. The profanity he's using is loud and clear. As I'm about to open the door, notations on a flip-chart behind Jack causes me to stop. The words "ICD vs. BILL LEE" are written in big, bright red letters. "Damnit, Jack's turned against me," I whisper.

Next I hear gunfire coming from above. One shot, followed seconds later by another, cause my little body to jump. The sounds of the blasts are deep, most likely from a shotgun. Near the stairwell I see Rich Farley, the mass murderer, slowly making his way toward me. Dressed in battle fatigues, he is holding a shotgun on one arm; on his left side, he's hoisting a boom box radio on his shoulder.

"You're supposed to be in San Quentin on death row!" I shout.

As I turn to run, a kid I got into a fight with as a teenager comes at me from the other end of the hall. He's holding a short club, tapping it against his palm. I charge at him swinging.

As I'm landing my punches, he's screaming...but it's a woman's voice. What the hell's going on? I wonder.

"Help! Wake up! Help! Wake up!" the voice continues.

I suddenly realize I'm punching my wife, in bed next to me. My fists are clenched, I'm out of breath, and tears are streaming down my face. I'm disoriented and drenched in sweat.

"Are you awake now?" she yells from under the covers.

"Oh God, I'm so sorry, honey," I cry, putting my arms around

her. "Are you alright?"

"I'm okay...I'm okay," she replies. "That was another bad one, huh?"

"It sure was," I answer, as she turns to hold me. "In fact, it was a two-parter."

It has taken a lot of courage for my wife to sleep with me, night after night, rolled up in a ball to protect herself. I don't know how she puts up with me. Lately, the nightmares have increased. Even after all these years, flashbacks of my dark past continue to haunt me. They say that time heals, but the intensity remains fresh and raw.

PART ONE

CHAPTER 1.

CHINATOWN'S DIRTY SECRETS

Children love their parents unconditionally and naturally seek their approval. In the Chinese culture, we're taught as children to honor and obey our parents—no matter what. I never doubted my mother and father's love for my siblings and me. But in our home, the most horrible acts conceivable against children were also committed.

We never knew the exact age of my father. He was born in *Toishan* (Southern China) around 1908 into the Yee family. Due to severe financial hardships in his family, my father was sold as a young boy to Mr. Chin Wai and raised as his "No. 1 Son," Chin Bork Ngai.

The brokering of sons was common in Toishan, where many families were impoverished. Children, especially "sons," were regarded as valuable commodities. Couples with financial resources who were not able to bear male infants resorted to this practice in order to carry on the family legacy. Daughters were also sold. The lucky ones became servants, while others were sexually exploited.

My mother once shared with me that Grandpa Yee was a heavy gambler, which was the source of the family's problems. My father never talked about his birth parents, and we were supposed to pretend that the Yee family never existed. My mother said that although *Ah Yeh* (Grandpa Chin) provided a comfortable, loving home, my father never forgave his biological parents for giving him up.

The only time my father cried was in his sleep, when he would scream like a little boy in anger at Grandpa Yee for not wanting him. Once, when I was about ten, I ran to him and held him as he sobbed in his sleep. As my father awoke, he pushed me away and pretended everything was fine.

He loved Ah Yeh and his eyes gleamed when he spoke of *Ngen Ngen* (Grandma Chin), who spoiled and showered him with affection. Two other boys were born into the Chin household, which also included servants.

My father was well-educated and studied medicine in Guangzhou, the capital of Guangdong (Canton) province. Two large picture frames hung in our living room containing degrees and certificates he received in China. In 1949, Ah Yeh, like many other wealthy landowners, had his land and assets seized by the Communists. My father was sent to Hong Kong, an embittered man, who later devoted a good part of his life serving the Kuomintang Nationalist Party. There just had to be a way for him to get back at the Communists, who destroyed his home and family.

My mother's childhood is a puzzle and contains many secrets. Born and raised in Guangzhou, Chu Lau Han was the eldest of three. Her father was an acclaimed educator who built and directed a university in Guangzhou.

My mother idolized *Ghown Ghown* (Grandpa Chu) as her hero, yet not a word was ever spoken about *Paw Paw* (Grandma Chu). When I inquired about her, my mother never responded.

At times, when my father became drunk and argued with my mother, he'd say, *"You're turning into your mother."*

She would either become silent and take it as a low blow, or snap back with something implying, *You will never be the man my father was.*

No matter how angry any of the kids became, we knew better than to bring up the subject of Paw Paw to hurt my mother. That would have been a death wish.

My mother was fluent in at least three dialects of Chinese, including Mandarin. She was tutored by Ghown Ghown, completing her studies at his university. She was cared for by a nanny and, like my father, had the luxury of servants.

When the Japanese invaded Guangzhou during the Sino-Japanese War, Ghown Ghown remained at his university while Paw Paw escaped with the children. Grandma Chin died unexpectedly, and my mother, who was nine at the time, became the caretaker for her baby brother and sister. They marched over a hundred miles to safety. The period from that time until she met my father, remains a mystery.

A number of possibilities have crossed my mind. *Perhaps Paw Paw was raped and murdered by soldiers. Could my mother have been abused in some way by soldiers or an acquaintance?* One thing was clear, she didn't trust anyone—not my father, her children, or even herself.

The marriage of my parents was arranged. My mother had settled in Hong Kong with her siblings, eventually reuniting with Ghown Ghown, who was indigent after the war. My father, twice married before meeting my mother, had five children. His first wife died after a short illness and he remarried almost immediately. When he arrived home unexpectedly one day, he walked in on wife "No. 2" brutally beating the children and banished her.

My father first entered the United States in 1939 as a "paper son." Ah Yeh found a way around the Chinese Exclusion Act by arranging for a merchant with a surname of Lee to sponsor my father as his son. My father returned to China in '49 to take another bride, as the Communists were dominating the country. With his five children scattered and cared for by various relatives, my father was seeking a better life in *Gum Shan*, or Gold Mountain (as California with its gold prospects was named by the Chinese).

Chu Lau Han, a beautiful woman with baby cheeks, fair skin and a mischievous smile, was eighteen when a matchmaker approached Ghown Ghown to discuss the prospects of a marriage and an opportunity to live in Gum Shan. The expectation, of course, was for the eldest to pave the way for the remaining Chu clan to join her in America.

As Ghown Ghown weighed the factors, the couple's age difference of more than twenty years was an issue. My father's two prior marriages and five children were also considerations. The Communists' takeover had left him financially ruined. But in the end, Grandpa Chu could not pass up the opportunity for his Lau Han to emigrate to the U.S., so he gave his blessing.

My mother never had a boyfriend and knew nothing about men. She presumed Bork Ngai would love and adore her just like her father had. My mother was smitten with my father's handsome looks, self-confidence, and charming wit.

After one meeting, my mother and father were married in Hong Kong. It was early 1949. Their simple wedding included the traditional tea ceremony whereby my mother knelt in front of Ngen

Ngen (her future mother-in-law) with her head bowed down, graciously offering a cup of tea. This ritual is a subtle way of saying, *Please accept me into your family.* It establishes the superior role of the mother-in-law from the outset. I wonder what Ngen Ngen's thoughts were, as this was the third ceremony she had endured for her eldest son.

My mother was in turmoil. She did not want to leave Ghown Ghown again. Yet she never questioned his decisions. She had a responsibility to the family, and what she wanted wasn't important. But leaving her home again to travel thousands of miles with a stranger she just married meant facing life's challenges unprepared. She didn't even know how to cook.

My mother had no idea how difficult life would be for her. Although my father would become one of the most powerful and respected men in San Francisco's Chinatown, he was also an alcoholic, compulsive gambler, womanizer, and much worse.

The remaining Chu clan never set foot in America. Lau Han never saw her loving father again. Her siblings slowly became strangers.

Bork Ngai and Lau Han arrived in San Francisco by boat in 1949. The journey took twenty-three days. By 1954, my mother had borne three girls and a boy. Mary was the first born, followed by James, Dorothy and May. I was not yet in the picture.

My father worked out of the living room as a Chinese doctor and herbalist. Wood shelves against the kitchen wall were stacked with glass jars containing herbs in various forms: pill, bark, leaves, and powder. My mother, like many other immigrant women from China, worked as a seamstress. As frugal as they were, they were not able to make ends meet. Ah Yeh, who worked at a pawn shop where he also lived, helped as much as he could. Money had to be borrowed from friends.

When my mother unexpectedly became pregnant with me, my father decided to abort me. Applying his medicinal training, he concocted a mixture of herbs which he coerced my mother to ingest. His scheme failed. I was born on October 8, 1954, with serious birth and developmental defects. How they discharged me from the hospital as a healthy baby boy is a mystery.

Due to continuing poverty, my parents entered negotiations to sell me to a wealthy, childless couple. (This transaction would have been disguised as a private adoption. The brokering of children in China found its way to America.) However, a decision to keep me was apparently influenced by the emotional trauma my father endured as a child who was sold. The reality is that I would have been better off with another family.

Being left-handed was considered bad luck in our culture, so I was forced to eat and write with my right hand. Sharp taps to the knuckles served as reminders. My parents' resentment toward me was absorbed like a sponge.

Seven of us occupied a two-room apartment on the corner of Washington and Stockton streets, above *Fun Loy* restaurant in the heart of Chinatown. We didn't have a refrigerator, had to heat our water on the stove and we shared beds. It was a typical ghetto tenement. Peeling paint dangled from the ceilings, hallways were morose and smelled of urine, and roaches outnumbered us at least a thousand-to-one.

There were twelve apartments in the building, and of course everyone knew everyone else's business. There was screaming and fighting heard regularly in the halls, but no other family could match the drama we dished out. An unwritten code existed in the building: no matter what was seen or heard, everyone stayed indoors and kept to themselves.

You can be sure that when we ran into the neighbors, the question, *"How is everything?"* was never asked. Instead, it was usually *"Sic fon may ah?"* (Have you eaten yet?) The polite response was, *"Sic bhow la."* (Ate plentifully.)

Before I was even a year old, a fire began in the kitchen of the restaurant below. Smoke came bellowing into our apartment late at night. My mother grabbed James and Dorothy while my father brought me and May out. Mary was left in the apartment until one of the restaurant workers courageously ran in and carried her to safety. The flames were minimal but the smoke was potentially deadly.

At age four, I became ill with severe abdominal pains. My father didn't trust Western doctors and refused to seek help. By the time he carried me into the hospital, my appendix had burst and my body was stricken with peritonitis poisoning. The medical staff informed my parents that the prognosis was grim.

As I lay near death, I visualized my mother standing and crying in a room. I was able to describe the room and surgical equipment. We discovered later that the details were precise, except that she was down the hall in another area away from me.

I remember encountering a spirit and the beautiful, serene sensation that encompassed it. The spirit encouraged me to follow him, but I refused. He expressed concerns about the hardships that lay ahead in my life. I told him I couldn't bear to leave my mother. I would come to regret that decision. The horrors that I eventually faced throughout life later convinced me that the spirit was trying to save me from hell on earth.

Years later, during one of many close encounters with death I faced, it occurred to me that at age four, I only spoke Cantonese. So how did the spirit and I communicate? Evidently, it wasn't through conventional language.

Frank Choy, a bright, bold surgeon, was the physician on call. He performed an emergency appendectomy, miraculously saving my life. My stomach was pumped and tubes were inserted into my leg to draw the toxicity from my body. I spent a terrifying month in the hospital.

During recovery, my father again endangered my life. Still convinced that he could provide better treatment, he abducted me from the hospital. The result was a high fever and infection which sent me back to the intensive care unit. Dr. Choy was infuriated and threatened my father with criminal action.

"Are you trying to kill your son, Mr. Chin?!" If you continue jeopardizing his life, I'll bring you up on charges!"

My father reluctantly behaved himself.

It was discovered during my hospitalization that I had serious congenital heart defects. Major enlargement and a loud murmur indicated ventricle dysfunction. Of course, the doctors were shocked that it was overlooked at birth. I was referred to the Department of Cardiology at the University of California-San Francisco Medical Center.

Once a month, I was examined by their top cardiologists, all of whom were Caucasian. The doctors were the first non-Asian people I had encountered. It was terrifying for me to be touched and probed by strangers with bright-colored hair and eyes. I used to break free from my mother's hold and run down the hospital corridor screaming at the top of my lungs. I was also convinced the electrocardiogram pads placed on my chest would electrocute me. Surgery was put off until I was older and able to withstand the procedure.

My mother had to take time out for my appointments. She had a way of making sure I knew the burden my health problems placed on her. During the long bus rides to the medical center, she never said a word. My mother just sighed all the way, at times choosing to sit away from me. I felt bad for being so much trouble.

My mother's resentment of taking me to the doctors and hospitals may have been due in part to guilt. She shared with one of my sisters that she blamed herself more than my father for my health problems. She felt it was her responsibility to protect me during her pregnancy.

In the ensuing years, I required numerous hospitalizations and surgeries. My other siblings, however, enjoyed good health. The botched abortion attempt had long-term ramifications on my well-being and development.

A non-profit charitable organization took up my cause and covered all the medical expenses for my treatments. They dropped our case after my father falsified information, putting me at risk again with no medical coverage. They gave him ample opportunities to cooperate but he refused. My father stood his ground, insisting that he was more than capable of treating me; that I didn't need those doctors. Years later, as I was hemorrhaging from a collapsed lung, my father finally admitted his shortcomings.

My father was obsessed with treating his children with herbs. Our tiny kitchen often reeked of strong, exotic fumes from the medicine brewing on the stove. Our bowel movements were monitored and laxatives "loosely" prescribed.

My mother didn't exactly sit still for his medical antics. After my father pressured her into attempting to abort me, she second-guessed all his diagnoses and consulted her own internist. She accused my father of being a quack who purchased his diplomas. That went really well with him. All the kids in the family learned to be skilled mediators for our parents.

My mother was emotionally unstable. Her fears were aggravated by my father's infidelity, which he denied, but was guilty of.

She attempted suicide on several occasions. Once we (the kids) had to break the bathroom door down and stop her as she began slashing her wrists. On several occasions, we had to restrain her from jumping out the window. I constantly worried that one day she might decide to take us out with her.

My mother had a hope chest that stored her prize possessions. From time to time, she showed off some of the beautiful sweaters she collected in her homeland. My sisters assumed that one day they'd have the privilege of wearing them.

One Friday afternoon, Mary came home to prepare for her eighth-grade graduation dance. None of us had anything resembling dress clothes, so Mary opened the hope chest. She put on one of Mommy's fancy sweaters.

"If Mommy was home, she'd say yea, huh?" Mary asked.

None of us responded. My mother was unpredictable in many ways. We all knew there was some risk involved.

Mary thought about running down to the sewing factory to get permission but there wasn't time. So off she went to the dance wearing the beautiful sweater.

We sat and crossed our fingers, praying that Mary would return first and put the sweater back without notice. Unfortunately, it didn't turn out that way. My mother came home and I held my breath.

I will never forget the look on my mother's face when Mary walked in wearing the sweater. It was as if the devil came through the door. My sister knew right away that she was in big trouble.

"Mommy, please don't be angry...I was wrong," she cried.

My mother charged toward Mary and yanked the sweater off. Mary started balling. For the next few minutes, my mother screamed at the top of her lungs as my sister cried harder and harder. Finally my mother sat down. Her entire body was convulsing from anger. I just stood there, with my mouth open. The only sound was Mary weeping.

Without looking away from the table, my mother spoke up. I didn't recognize the voice; it was eerie.

"Bring me the scissors," she demanded.

"Mommy...Mommy...no...I'll never dare do this again. Go ahead and hit me," my sister pleaded through her tears.

I prayed that perhaps my mother was going to cut Mary's hair to punish her. But I knew it was going to be much worse. Mary begged and begged to be hit but my mother wasn't going to let her off that easily. At that point, I think each of us would have been willing to take a beating for Mary.

Finally, Mary brought the scissors to my mother. She carefully laid the material out and just like that, the beautiful sweater was sheared into pieces.

"Is there anything else you'd like to wear of mine?" she shouted.

I thought my mother was going to snip everything in the chest but she didn't. Her reaction toward Mary left me with the impression that although we were her children, she also perceived us as her enemies. She was a master at making us feel repulsive.

My mother was also paranoid, repeatedly warning us that one day our father would *"soct say ngor ga."* (kill us all.) After a while, I kept a large knife under my mattress, not for fear of intruders, but to protect myself from my own family. In my mind, it was perfectly clear: the world is not a safe place.

By age eight, I was suffering from OCD (Obsessive Compulsive Disorder). I didn't know what it was or what to do. I washed my hands uncontrollably, often till they bled. I couldn't stand being touched, and everything had to be done in a specific order.

I found myself counting the number of times my eyes blinked as well as the number of breaths I took. My dad and brother tormented me about it. I was also preoccupied with death. I was convinced I had a terminal illness and obsessed with the fear of my parents dying.

A small box containing baseball cards and a ping-pong ball was meticulously stored in a drawer. When all hell broke loose in the house, I went into my special box and rearranged it. I felt the only thing I had control of in the world was in that box.

Violence was common in our home. It was easy to provoke my father after he got drunk, which occurred nightly. James, who is four years older, brutalized me for years. Perhaps he felt compelled to take on the role of man of the house and didn't know how to maintain control, resorting to constantly beating the "shit" out of my sister, May and me in order to rule his domain. Talk back or get in his way and I'd find myself with a bloody nose. My arms and legs were twisted to the brink of snapping. As I lay on the floor in tears, the savage would suddenly become a charmer, concerned about what he had done. James decided he should be forgiven. Because I reserved the right to stay angry, another beating was administered.

Dorothy never talked back and did whatever you asked. Mary was the eldest and James respected her. I was so distraught, I often thought of strangling or stabbing him while he slept. He finally left May alone when she dug her nail into his face during a scuffle, scarring him permanently. I witnessed it and felt a sense of redemption. He left me alone after I kicked him in the groin, but it wasn't enough for me. As we got older, my repressed anger still needed to be released on him. The years of abuse were far from being settled.

My father never beat the boys, but he sure took things out on my sisters. He would make a fist, then push the index and middle fingers out. With the knuckles of those fingers protruding, he would smash them against their heads. Chinese refer to the disciplinary blow as a *ling gawk*. In our house, my father frequently administered his ling gawks during dinner.

The seating arrangement at our makeshift dining table illustrated our family hierarchy. My father sat at one end and I was on the opposite side. Clockwise, my father was at the top of the table, followed by my mother, James, me, May and finally Dorothy. Mary was smart. She began working in her early teens and had an excuse for missing family meals.

My father was quiet when dinner started, but after a few drinks, he turned into a monster. Bottles of bourbon and whiskey were placed on the floor by his feet. We'd start giggling and he would demand silence. Outbursts continued with Dorothy receiving all the beatings. She sat on my father's right. Her head was in his direct line of fire. When she cried, it provoked him further. Often, Dorothy would arrive early and sit away from my father, but the seating order was dictated by him and not to be questioned.

I could usually tell when he was about to "go off." Not only would he give you the evil eye, but his jaw muscles would pulsate rapidly. I tried warning my sisters, but they never saw it coming. Dorothy got hit once for staring at my father's jaw.

Eventually, the rest of us boycotted the table and left my father eating alone. We scurried when he got up from the table. Once he slept it off for about half-an-hour, he was mellow again. Then he couldn't wait to get out of the house.

My father always dashed out after dinner. So I followed him out the door and tagged along wherever he went. As a child, I relished those times together, as they provided an opportunity for me to bond with him. For better or worse, I longed to be with him.

He was quite involved in Chinatown politics and an active member in the Kuomintang Nationalist Party. There were a lot of boring meetings. Yet, my eyes would light up when he spoke. No matter how abusive my father was toward me, I still idolized him.

The KMT sponsored a Chinese language school in its headquarters, and my father taught there part-time. It was just a block from our house. In time, he was elected principal of the school. This is one of the most prestigious positions to hold in the KMT and the community. Education has always been highly valued in our culture, so teachers, especially principals, are held in the highest regard.

Although my father repeatedly swore to my mother that he was broke, he always seemed to have money for gambling and drinking. We spent most nights in mah-jong parlors—not the most conducive environment for a small child, with their scrappy furniture, smoke-filled rooms, ivory tiles clanging and players screaming profanities at one another. *"Dill nay ga lo mo"* (Fuck your mother) and *"kai dai"* (bastard) were hurled across the tables. I usually slept on the couch or floor until the wee hours. I anticipated arguments when my mother accompanied my father. One or both would lose and take it out on the other.

After I started kindergarten, it was just my father and me at the nightly mah-jong games. I had to keep an eye out for him since he'd be in a stupor from the alcohol as we walked through Chinatown after dinner. When he fell, there wasn't much I could do.

"*Daddy, hey sun*" (get up), I pleaded, while yanking on his arm. It was quite embarrassing as he was a well-known figure in the community. People who stopped and offered to help felt sorry for me. They were often more concerned about me than my father.

My father allocated time between dinner and mah-jong for my Tai Chi lessons. I wanted to study karate at the YMCA, but my father insisted on teaching me martial arts himself. The lingering effects of the alcohol on him made the effort quite frustrating. We used the assembly hall in KMT headquarters, which was filled with photographs of Sun Yat Sen, Chiang Kai Shek, and other forefathers of the Republic of China. An elderly janitor was usually there, cleaning up.

It was quite hilarious if you can picture the two of us in identical poses with our arms extended and legs bent, staring at each other. We would be stuck because "Master Daddy" couldn't remember the next sequence of moves. I was forbidden to question his instruction and struggled not to laugh. Eventually, the janitor initiated a ritual of practicing Tai Chi next to us. I had to sneak a peek at him in order to rescue my father from our predicament. That old janitor must have had many a good laugh on us.

"*Ah Chell, jow-la*" (Son, it's time to go), my father would say, waking me up when the mah-jong game ended. As we walked home, I could tell by the way he held my hand if he had won or lost. When he won, I received a percentage of the winnings, so we were essentially gambling partners. Our ritual was to pick up sil-yeh (late-night snack) at Sam Wo's on the way home. When my father lost, the walk seemed a lot longer. I went straight to bed and left him sitting alone, which he preferred.

My father was not exactly the best role model. My mother taught us to do the right thing, while my father was extremely dishonest. He lived by his own rules. He bullied people and believed in screwing the other guy first. Basically, my father lived on the dark side.

One day at a hardware store in Chinatown, I followed and watched him stroll from aisle to aisle, where he stuffed a measuring tape, paint brushes and putty knives in his coat pockets. My father walked up to the counter and paid for a piece of sandpaper. Everything was sticking out of his pockets. He had total disregard for his crime, and the proprietor didn't dare confront him. Of course I had to promise not to tell my mother. We had an understanding that my mother was never to be told anything.

———

I had my first job even before starting kindergarten shining shoes for ten cents. My brother and I ventured to Saint Mary's Square Park in Chinatown and worked afternoons and weekends, shining shoes till dark. On good days, businessmen handed us quarters in appreciation of our efforts.

Unfortunately, we also had to be wary of men in the park trying to lure us with money to satisfy their sick urges. We didn't know what pedophiles were back then, only that these men, who approached us with devious stares, had to be avoided and dealt with. They were labeled *Hom Sup Low* (Dirty Old Men). At times, we turned to older street kids for assistance. We baited the weirdoes into an alley and beat the shit out of 'em. They were robbed for good measure. This was never reported, not even to our parents. I accepted early on that there were bad people and lots of secrets in Chinatown. One learns quickly about survival on the streets.

Categorizing us as latchkey kids would be an understatement. Lacking supervision and a sense of right or wrong, we passed our time stealing, fighting and gambling. We climbed roof-tops, scaled elevator shafts and played cat-and-mouse with the police. Most of the activities involved high-risk behavior which we carried into our teens and adulthood.

With barely enough money to keep food on the table, my mother insisted that we attend Saint Mary's Catholic School, half a block from our home. The tuition alone was nearly half of what my mother earned at the garment factory. She wasn't religious but wanted us to learn good values. My mother was also concerned about a busy intersection we'd have to cross in order to attend the public school, so the location on our same side of the street provided her with peace of mind.

I do not have fond memories of grammar school. Because Chinese was my only language at the time, I struggled in school from the start. Placed with the lowest academic group in classes, I was labeled stupid. The aptitude tests in English were foreign to me. Most of my classmates were third-generation Chinese-Americans and didn't understand my difficulties. Of course, most of them were monolingual. The only Chinese they knew was *Gung Hay Fat Choy,* which got them "lucky money" for New Year's. I was already fluent in three dialects of Chinese by the time I enrolled in school.

In our home, we spoke *Sam Yup* (Cantonese) and *Sze Yup* (Toishan dialect). I picked up the third dialect, *Lhong Dhown,* from friends at the playground.

As a young child, I also suffered from an eating disorder. I disliked most food and was fixated on rice and peanuts. Night after night, that's all I ate. During lunch at Saint Mary's, which was served in a basement auditorium, we were required to clean off our plates. Initially forced to eat, which caused me to vomit, I finally refused. My punishment was loss of recess privileges. Student-hostesses assigned to my table resented me, as I caused each of them demerits.

Jason Fung and Frank Lau were my best friends. Both were recent immigrants from Hong Kong. Frank was the strong, gutsy one; Jason was tall and shy; I was known as the conniving one. We spoke Cantonese among ourselves and did everything together. We even went to the bathroom together. The three of us would stand around the commode and pee at the same time, crisscrossing our streams. We didn't have any hang-ups about silly things like that.

All of us came from troubled homes and endured similar pains. I shared secrets with them that I never trusted anyone else with. We discussed fears about our homes and lives; whether God approved of us. We talked seriously about running away together. We were only in second grade. Who could have guessed all of us would end up in gangs, and one of us would be convicted of murder.

I got into fights almost daily. Sometimes, it seemed as though I spent more time in Principal Sister Mildred's office, getting paddled, than in class. A pale-skinned, tiny woman with folds of wrinkle hanging out of her habit, she grind her teeth and grunted as she delivered each blow. Initially, her rage shocked me. Soon, I accepted her as disturbed, just like me. I knew that it was only a matter of time before I grabbed the paddle and turned it on her.

The worst time for me in school was during Open House. We were required to sit at our desks whether our parents attended or not. My father and mother never participated in school activities. I think my oldest sister Mary and I took it the hardest. It was torture for me to sit up straight with my hands neatly clasped on the desk, with my tests and class assignments neatly piled on the top right corner. I'd stare at the door and prayed that my parents would show up—they never did. They were usually the only parents missing. There was a lot of resentment acted out the next day in the schoolyard. I attacked anyone who teased me about my parents' absence.

I attended St. Mary's for eight years, including two years in the third grade. My brother and I were out of control, and they held us back together. We broke all their records for truancy, fighting and stealing. Corporal punishment didn't deter us. The most difficult transition I faced in staying behind my class was the friendships. I gradually became distant from Jason and Frank. New friendships had to be established with kids who were a year younger. I never really clicked with anyone except a kid named Winston.

After I completed the sixth grade, my parents gave in to my pleas, allowing me to transfer to public school. In private, Sister Mildred made it clear to me that I was not welcomed back the following year. That suited me fine. I couldn't wait to get out of there. I swore to go after that "old penguin." She treated me like I was possessed by the devil. When I left St. Mary's, my belief in God and religion was abandoned as well.

CHAPTER 2.
CHINESE PLAYGROUND

The city of San Francisco purchased the land in 1925 and completed construction in 1927. The playground was situated with Waverly Alley to the east, Hang Ah Alley to the west, and Clay and Sacramento streets as its north and south borders, respectively. There were three levels within the grounds. A basketball court was on the lower level, and a tennis and volleyball court were in the upper section. Everything was out in the open. A small clubhouse with a pagoda design stood on the main level along with a slide, swings, merry-go-round, and ring apparatus.

I spent countless hours playing ping pong on a table that was bolted to the ground in front of the clubhouse. Every few years, they'd slap a new table-top on. Behind the building sat a mini-slide and concrete sandbox where we transported water for our *muddy-duddy* creations.

There were three ways to enter and exit the park: from the two alleys and on Sacramento Street. The multiple accesses served us well as children playing hide-and-seek. The playground was our home base and we hid throughout Chinatown.

As a young boy, I was chased by the police in one entrance and out the other over illegal fireworks sales or other petty crimes.

The first gang of immigrant kids, the *Wah Chings,* originated out of this playground in 1964, complete with club jackets. They discreetly came in and out through Waverly Alley and congregated in the basketball court that they used for soccer. Every Sunday afternoon, an organized volleyball game was played in which gang members participated with others from their homeland.

The gang wars from the late sixties to late seventies turned the playground into a hot spot. It symbolized the ruling gang in Chinatown, and opposing sides ambushed one another at all entrances. Chinese Playground was a second home to me from the time I was a toddler. Just half a block from our house, it was reached by crossing one intersection to Hang Ah Alley. Kids gathered there early in the day on weekends, holidays and during the summer. We also played in alley ways, jumped on and off moving cable cars and hung around department stores downtown. But at the end of each day, we regrouped at the playground.

Paul Whang was the site director there throughout my childhood. An affable man, he befriended my siblings and me. One evening, he showed up at our home and presented my sister Mary with a brand new dictionary.

"Mr. and Mrs. Lee, Mary's a bright girl and always pleasant to be around. I know she'll put this to good use."

My mother and father gleamed from embarrassment. Paul wasn't fluent in Chinese, so my parents had difficulty understanding him. Still, they knew he was making a kind, generous gesture. His gift brought tears to my sister's eyes.

Most of the kids who hung out at the playground spent more time with Paul than with their own parents. He was firm, yet highly skilled in diplomacy, earning respect from *fei jies* (gangsters) who were fearless. Paul eventually brought in a young fella named Dougie to be his assistant.

Bored, restless and perhaps self-destructive, we didn't use the playground apparatus as it was intended. When Paul and Dougie weren't around, we climbed high up the poles atop the equipment, leaped off the giant swings in mid-air, scaled fences and played tag on the clubhouse's shingled roof. Every so often, someone fell and ended up in the hospital, returning with a cast on their arm or leg. It was pure luck we didn't get ourselves killed.

We climbed all over Chinatown. One kid climbing over a gate at Commodore Stockton school slipped; the tapered point on one of the iron bars pierced straight through his thigh.

Once my brother and I were throwing rocks at cars from our rooftop, and a driver came after us with his buddies. We hid by standing behind a wood fence on a narrow ledge five stories above ground with nothing to hang on to. I held my breath and closed my eyes for dear life. Jumping across rooftops also gave me "rushes."

The playground was our headquarters for selling fireworks. Compared to shining shoes at the park for ten cents, this was much more lucrative, and in our minds, worth the risks. We hid packs and cases (bricks) of firecrackers in the bushes, the sandbox and even under the merry-go-round. Then we positioned ourselves on the perimeter of Chinatown to solicit sales—Grant Avenue from Bush to California; the intersection of Washington and Kearny; even Pacific and Columbus Avenues, bordering North Beach. The cable car stops, streets near the freeway exit ramps and other main roads leading into Chinatown were also prime locations for us to pitch our wares on weeks preceding the Fourth of July.

Out-of-town customers drove up, rolled down their windows, paid for and received their merchandise, then went on their way. You can say we offered drive-thru service. Some of us peddled during Chinese New Year's, but the demand for fireworks was much greater for the Fourth of July.

An informal cooperative existed among the dealers, and prices were established by consensus (price-fixing). Individuals deviating and undercutting to generate sales were beaten up and ostracized.

We used the same supplier, shared information on police undercover operations and teamed up to split large sales. When a dealer had his fireworks confiscated by the cops, the rest of us chipped in to replenish his stash in order to cushion the loss. There was no need to be greedy. We realized that the more we worked together and honored our "code," the higher the profits for everyone.

We also protected one another when there was trouble. Anyone trying to rip one of us off wouldn't make it out of Chinatown. Everyone dropped what they were doing and went after the perpetrator. Cocky, smart-assed outsiders were also beaten up and robbed of their money.

The older dealers preferred selling in large volumes and pushing stronger explosives such as cherry and barrel bombs (M-80s). They intimidated the younger white kids which created a market for me. I was content making my money selling individual packs.

In the early 60's, when I started in the business, I paid six cents for a pack that contained sixteen firecrackers. I turned around and sold them for twenty-five cents (individual firecrackers were sold for five cents), turning a good profit. Five years later, my costs remained the same but I doubled my selling price to fifty cents per pack.

I learned from shining shoes that building rapport with customers was an integral part of business. Whether polishing wing-tips or selling packs of firecrackers, it helped for me to stand out among my competitors. Clients who preferred to deal with me were a testimonial that they trusted and enjoyed doing business with me.

Trust is important in the black market. We used aliases and mine was Ron. (I never liked my name—William Lee; too common. It didn't seem to fit me.) When kids came into the playground and asked specifically for Ron, it made me feel special.

Part of our code was keeping the playground preserved as our sanctuary. We never completed transactions on the grounds. Customers were kept or escorted at least a block away and waited as we retrieved the goods. After the police questioned me in the park one day, we didn't hide our fireworks there any longer.

Officer Al spent most of his career patrolling Chinatown and we despised him. A Caucasian man who stood around five-ten, he had a mustache and tanned complexion from his constant exposure to the sun. His uniform was loose and wrinkled; the sleeves were always rolled up, even under his rain gear in winter.

After intercepting one of my sales, two undercover officers chased me through the streets but I eluded them. The next day, Al came looking for me at the playground. I was sitting alone on a bench and watched as he and his partner entered from different directions to thwart my chances of fleeing. The thought never crossed my mind to make a run for it. There was no reason to. I was expecting them.

"Okay, son, stand up and put your arms out," he commanded.

"What's this about?" I asked, remaining seated.

"Look, don't get smart with me," he shouted. "Do I have to drag you up?"

Slowly getting up, I extended both arms out to my sides. Methodically, he went through all my pockets: pants, shirt, jacket, even searched my shoes. He came up empty-handed.

"Your name is Ron, right?" he asked.

"Nope," I replied.

"Aw, come on," he said in disgust. "Don't play with me. We took some firecrackers from a kid the other day and he said you sold it to him. He told us all about you, Ron."

"I know my name, man," I said sarcastically. "It ain't Ron and I don't know nothin' about selling firecrackers."

Right then, Paul approached us. He had known Al for years and they respected one another.

"What's up over here, guys?" Paul asked calmly. "How's it going, Al?"

"Paul, do you know this kid?" Al asked.

"Sure, I do. That's William Lee. I know his entire family. He's a good kid."

"Well, we think he's been selling fireworks, robbing kids and causing trouble with my fellow officers."

"Oh no, that can't be," Paul exclaimed. "William, have you been doing what the officer says?"

"No way," I answered.

"Alright, we didn't find anything on you and you're lucky Paul is here. But I'm going to keep a close eye on you—you understand?!"

I didn't respond. After the officers left, Paul turned and walked me into the clubhouse with his arm around my shoulder.

"That's it, young man...your selling days are over," he whispered.

As I entered the clubhouse, I waited for Paul to go into his office. On a chair in the corner rested the jacket that I had worn to the playground. I was wearing the spare that I kept there for situations like this. I had switched jackets when I arrived earlier. If Al had searched my regular jacket, he would have found packs of firecrackers, money, a knife and a pass-key. Each pocket was laced with gunpowder residue. That was enough for them to haul me away.

I heeded Paul's warning, out of respect for him and in compliance with the code. Anyone busted or bringing heat to the business retired for the season. It's for their own good and to avoid provoking the cops.

Officer Al hassled quite a few of us that year. One day, we made an effigy of him littered with profanities. The doll was stuffed in a crate originally packed with fireworks and marked accordingly. It was placed in the bushes for Al to find. After discovering the decoy, he reached in and pulled out his effigy. I'll never forget the infuriating look on his face. Even his partner was grinning behind Al's back. Hiding behind a car across the street, I laughed so hard I began rolling on the ground and almost pee'd in my pants.

Looking back, I see that the playground wasn't a conducive place for any child to be. Adults who chaperoned their children there enjoyed the facility as it was intended. But it was, for the most part, comprised of kids from troubled homes thrown together, unsupervised. Paul was a good influence, but he was one person. Junior sociopaths outnumbered him twenty to one.

We didn't develop the right social skills at Chinese Playground. The environment represented the dark side. We learned to cheat and lie. What you could get away with prevailed over fair play. It was "screw the other guy first" and "you don't let anyone fuck with you." Conflict resolution meant throwing the first punch. We were overly sensitive, hostile and aggressive. Revenge was always sweet; that's how you earned respect.

I learned to hide my emotions at the playground. Fear was a sign of weakness and humor was usually at the expense of someone else. Our days were filled with "dares" and ridicule. Any sign of vulnerability was callously exploited.

A lot of fights took place behind the clubhouse and usually went unnoticed. You "called someone down" (challenged them to fight), and everyone headed over to watch. Even if you didn't want to, you had to fight, or never step foot in the playground again. There were times when I was so frightened, I threw the first punch so my friends wouldn't notice my knees shaking. After a while, it was no big deal. I started fights in order to save face because someone was perceived to be making me look bad, or to gain respect with other kids. I pretended that blows didn't hurt by ignoring the pain or by faking it.

I was lucky to have older siblings there looking out for me. My sister Dorothy, though, was sweet and gentle. She was easy-going and wouldn't hurt a fly. Her passive demeanor was targeted one day and she got pushed around. She was thirteen at the time.

My sister Mary went ballistic. She got her girlfriends together and taught the other girl and her cohorts a good lesson. The retaliation also served as a warning to others that Dorothy was not to be messed with.

We learned street etiquette and survival from the older kids, who were mentored by those before them. I was bullied and naturally became one. Unfortunately, some of the situations were a bit too much for a young child to cope with.

One Sunday morning while many of my friends were in Church, I was playing alone near the swings and noticed something in the sand. It was a folded wallet, light brown in color, with a rodeo cowboy on a bucking horse etched on one side; a zipper ran along the edges.

The clubhouse was not yet opened. Unbuttoning my shirt at the waist, I quickly tucked the wallet inside against my elbow and ran home. *Finders keepers...losers weepers...finders keepers...losers weepers,* I chanted all the way. *There could be a fortune in here...I'm rich! I'm rich!*

Entering the hallway of my apartment building, I peeked in the wallet. A person's name, address and phone number were visible through a plastic compartment. It read, Donald Jew. Spreading the billfold apart, I pulled out two one-dollar bills and a five-dollar bill. *Yes! Yes!*

I was so excited I ran in the apartment and smack into my mother.

"Oops! Hello Mommy," I said, bouncing off her as I hid my treasure.

"You're back so early?" she asked.

"Mmm," I acknowledged.

No older than nine at the time, I spent the next twenty minutes tormenting myself. Initially ecstatic about squandering the money, I became consumed with guilt as my mother performed her chores in front of me. Reminding myself of the sacred values she instilled in us, I realized how disappointed she'd be with me for keeping the money. *Too bad Daddy wasn't home,* I thought. *He'd probably encourage me to keep the money.*

Approaching her with the wallet, I reluctantly handed it to her.

"Mommy, I found this at the playground. There's seven dollars in it."

"What a Good boy. Now, you go back and turn it in to Paul."

Unfortunately, my good intentions became complicated, as things at Chinese Playground had a way of turning into hard lessons.

Upon my return, the clubhouse was open. As I walked in, Victor, someone I normally stayed away from, greeted me. About nineteen, he was lanky, had dark complexion, slicked his hair back, and always dressed to impress. Victor had a pointed chin with a deep one-inch scar that ran underneath the center and he strutted around like a rooster. Victor dropped out of high school, drank and hustled on the streets; overall, one bad dude.

"What's up, little man?" he asked.

"Is Paul here?"

"Nah, it's Sunday, man. Dougie's here. He'll be right back. What 'cha got there?" he asked, staring at the wallet in my hand.

"Oh, I found this near the swings...I want to turn it in."

"Aah man, just give it to me," he insisted. "I'll give it to him."

No way, I told myself.

But I didn't really have a choice. On the streets, "shining on" or ignoring his request would be considered disrespectful. He stood staring down at me with his beady, penetrating eyes. I didn't have anything to prove and wasn't expected to act tough; not when it came to someone bigger and older.

"Alright," I said, handing it to him.

Staying put for a few seconds, I prayed for Dougie to walk in. Finally, I left as Victor became agitated with me.

Running up the stairs, I hid behind some branches on the edge of the tennis court and staked out the clubhouse. Five minutes later, Dougie came out of the men's room and walked in. A minute later, Victor strolled out and exited on Sacramento Street. I ran to the end of the alley and watched as he disappeared onto Grant Avenue.

For ten minutes, I debated with myself about going back down. The safest thing to do was forget the whole wallet incident. But if my suspicions were correct, then my deed was meaningless and I'd be the victim as much as Donald Jew.

That's not right, man...no way! I thought. Slowly, I walked back down, step by step, and cautiously entered the building as I looked over my shoulder. I closed the door behind me and turned the bolt.

"What are you doing, William? I want the door open," Dougie said.

"I need to talk to you—it's important," I whispered. "I found a wallet this morning. Did you get it?"

"Yeah, it's right here. So *you* found it, eh?"

"Yep, I gave it to Victor. Is the money there?" I asked nervously.

"Money?! Victor said there wasn't any money."

"Shit!" I said.

"Wait a minute. You're saying there was money in there?" Dougie asked. "You know how much?"

"Yeah, seven dollars," I replied.

"Well, I'll be damned," Dougie said. "Okay, I'll take care of this. We'll get the money back from Victor. He and I are going to have a long talk."

"Am I going to get in trouble?" I asked. "What if he comes after me?"

"Don't you worry," he replied. "Just let me know if he makes any trouble."

Yeah, right, I thought. *That's if I get a chance.* His response didn't reassure me. He didn't say anything about ordering Victor to stay away from me.

Two days later, Victor grabbed me in the restroom and shoved me against the wall. There was another kid about my age in there, but that didn't deter him.

"Listen, you little punk!" he shouted. "You cost me seven dollars, so you owe me the money. You bring me the dough or you're dead. If you tell anyone, I'll kill you—you hear me! You should have kept your fuckin' mouth shut!"

With that, he whipped out a switchblade knife, flicked it open and pressed the long blade against my cheek. I thought I was going to be "shanked," right then and there.

I'd never been so frightened in my life. After Victor retracted the blade and left, I stood there heaving, too shocked to even cry. The other kid ran out of the bathroom. I was afraid to move. My heart was pounding so hard I thought it would explode.

Standing next to the urinal, with my back pressed against the filthy wall, I still felt the cold, sharp blade against my face.

At age nine, I had already witnessed plenty of violence, but this was directed at me, personally. *Who can I turn to?* I wondered. Everyone I knew was afraid of Victor, including my siblings. *Trying to do the right thing got me into the mess. If I went to Paul, Dougie would hate me. I shoulda' just kept the damn money.* My honest deed was going to get me killed. I knew I had to come up with the money, somehow. My life became a series of anxious days and sleepless nights. For nearly a week, I didn't dare leave the house alone. My compulsive hand-washing went totally "haywire." Nobody noticed.

Finally I confided in my father. I was afraid my mother would take me to the police, although most folks in Chinatown weren't known for reaching out to them. Chinese don't trust foreigners and their laws in general. Also, Chinese and Irish have a long history of hostility going back to the railroad days. When I was a child, the city's police force was heavily represented by Irish-Americans. I was taught to fear and distrust them. There was one Chinese cop in the entire department, and I'm almost sure he wasn't bilingual.

Serious conflicts among our countrymen are traditionally resolved through benevolent associations. These groups are organized by surname or geography (districts in China). The largest of these organizations make up the Chinese Six Companies, located a stone's throw from our house. Essentially, we take care of our own problems.

My father was teaching part-time at the Kuomintang headquarters on Stockton Street, and his office faced the playground. The following day, sitting there with him, I saw a friend of mine from the office window and called to him.

"Norm, what's up?" I shouted.

Running toward the window, he looked up and yelled, "Don't come down, William. That guy's here...Victor."

"Okay," I said.

I turned to my father. *"Daddy, he's there."*

Clearing his throat, my father picked up the phone and started turning the rotary dial. There was a click and someone answered.

"I'm at the school. You can come now," my father whispered.

Ten minutes later, a strange man appeared. Dressed in a suit without a tie, he was stocky and looked intense. His face didn't reveal any emotions. We weren't introduced.

My father instructed the man to accompany me to the playground. As we approached the entrance, the man stopped as Norm joined us.

Placing his hand on my shoulder, he said, *"You tell me who's the one bothering you..."*

"That's him," I replied, pointing to Victor through the fence, where he stood with his back to us.

"You go back to your father now," he said. *"You don't have to be afraid. You two should stay away from the playground for a few days. Do you understand?"*

We both nodded and ran off. That was it. I assumed the man was one of my father's mah-jong friends and he was going to speak with Victor and ask him to leave me alone.

Two days later, we heard Victor was in the hospital. Someone said he was beaten up by Tong (underworld) enforcers.

People whispered and speculated about what went down. I figured he had it coming. An eye for an eye, right? Part of me felt vindicated, but mainly, I was just glad he was out of my hair. I was curious, but knew better than to ask my father who that stranger was. And of course, it was another one of our secrets.

Shortly after Victor was discharged from the hospital, he enlisted in the Army. When Victor completed his basic training, he stopped by the playground before being transferred out. I walked in the clubhouse and was surprised to see him. When he saw me, he quickly turned and left.

Years later, Paul transferred to the Chinese "Rec" Center across from the cable car barn. As more immigrants arrived from Hong Kong and organized gangs began taking over the playground, American-born Chinese kids gradually headed over to Chinese Center. I hung out at both facilities, eventually spending more time with Paul and his new staff. But when the Fourth of July approached, you'd find me back at the playground. It remained the headquarters for our money-making operations.

There were more directors at the Chinese Center and they were very strict. I complained but welcomed the consistent, structured rules. It felt much safer there.

One of the assistant directors was a fella named Fred Lau. A no-nonsense type, he didn't let us get away with anything. Most of us were afraid of him. He applied to join the police department and successfully fought to change the minimum height requirement. As he rose through the ranks, I was motivated to stay out of trouble. Anything to avoid running into him. In 1995, Fred was appointed police chief of San Francisco, the first Asian in the city's history to hold that position.

CHAPTER 3.

KEEPING UP WITH THE WONGS

Ah Yeh (Grandpa Chin) was the most frugal person I've ever known. He didn't let anything go to waste. When we visited him at the pawn shop in Ross Alley, he took butcher paper, cut it into neat squares, punched holes along the margin and used old strings to bind them together. Just like that, we had our custom notebooks.

It was difficult picturing him in his big house in China staffed with servants. He never talked about the luxuries, nor did he complain about losing everything to the Communists. I wished he had expressed his emotions more.

I never saw him buy anything for himself, except food. He was quiet, yet authoritative. Although he never spanked us, I never doubted the possibility.

My father was adopted but their resemblance was remarkable. There were only a few people that my father respected, and Ah Yeh was one of them. My father was courteous and friendly to influential people in Chinatown, but I knew when he truly respected and honored someone.

Ah Yeh saved every penny he could and didn't trust banks. He hid money under his pillow and other obscured places. On a number of occasions, I had to help him search his living quarters because he forgot where his stashes were hidden. He panicked, screaming that he had been robbed, but the money always turned up.

I was seven when Ah Yeh passed away. He was eighty-three, the only grandparent I ever knew. We had a wake followed by a funeral the next day. After the wake, my father stayed alone with Ah Yeh at the funeral home; he just wanted to be with his father one last time.

Ah Yeh's death traumatized me as well as my brother. Sitting side by side as the funeral service began, James nudged me.

"You're not going to cry, right?" he whispered.

"What do you mean?" I asked.

"Come on...if you don't cry, I won't cry," he proposed. "Everyone's going to be staring at us if we cry."

I didn't know *how* I was going to behave. I knew I didn't want to be there. Ah Yeh's death puzzled me. Now, my brother was giving me an option.

"We have a deal," he insisted.

I looked up at my mother sitting to my right. She was too consumed with her own grief to know what we were up to.

Shortly after the services began, my brother started elbowing me and soon we were giggling. Then it got out of control. As other family members' weeping intensified, our laughter increased.

Surprisingly, my parents left us alone. I think they understood. I shared with my mother and father the night before that I was worried and scared for Ah Yeh. They tried to comfort me. They knew my brother and I loved him dearly and would never disrespect him intentionally.

Ah Yeh lying in the open casket terrified and confused me. I wanted him to wake up and comfort me; to pull me in against his lap and hold me like he always did when I was frightened.

When I was four, we went to a studio to take a family portrait. It is the only existing picture that includes Ah Yeh with us. I was scared out of my wits by the photographer and his equipment, especially the props. The picture, which sat atop the encyclopedia case in my mother's living room, shows a family with a frightened little boy leaning against his grandfather's lap. Next to Ah Yeh was the only spot I would stand still.

As soon as the funeral service ended and the casket was closed, I breached the pact my brother lured me into. I started crying my eyes out and screamed for Ah Yeh. I wanted to run and open the casket to free him. My mother had to restrain me. There was no more denying that he was gone, forever.

Ah Yeh was laid to rest in a cemetery with his countrymen from Toishan. After the burial, my father came home with a large portrait of Ah Yeh which we hung in our apartment. It offered some comfort for me that he was still watching over us.

The division of Ah Yeh's assets turned ugly. My two uncles and my father nearly came to blows over it. From what I recall, there were ill feelings regarding the amount of money each received, but a major point of contention occurred over money set aside for cemetery visits.

Chinese tradition places strong emphasis on honoring the dead. Paying homage to deceased relatives occurred twice a year (spring and fall). Flowers, food and alcohol are brought to the grave sites. This is referred to as *Bai Shan.*

My parents' version was that my uncles wanted to divide up the money Ah Yeh reserved for Bai Shan. Perhaps they weren't comfortable with my father controlling the fund. The disagreement led to my parents severing ties with my uncles.

The lack of documentation such as marriage and birth certificates has always created problems in the Chinese-American community when it comes to estate settlements. Disputes occur more often than people outside our culture realize, whether "wills" have been prepared or not. Outsiders presume Chinese always maintain strong family ties, but the truth is that greed and betrayal exist within our culture like any other. A number of attorneys I know in Chinatown who specialize in litigation believe problems actually occur more often among Chinese families.

There are umpteen stories of parents transferring property to their children, then finding themselves evicted.

My parents took the money they received from Ah Yeh, borrowed from friends, and purchased their first piece of property. It was a five-unit building on Nob Hill, an upscale San Francisco neighborhood, not far from Chinatown. There were three flats, a store with living quarters and a secluded rear apartment. Located a block from the Huntington Hotel and two blocks from the Fairmont, it was prime real estate.

When my parents first purchased the property, the rear apartment faced a concrete yard. My father immediately went to work, taking out the cement and filling the area with soil. He created a beautiful garden, performing all the labor with his own hands.

At school, when our curriculum required making oral reports to our classmates, I described the garden one day and brought a flower from one of my father's plants.

"My name is William Lee; room seven; grade four. We have a beautiful garden. My father built it. He broke the ground up and took everything out. Then he put in dirt. Now we have beautiful flowers there. I help him. I water the garden. This is from the garden. [I held out a rich multi-colored flower.] The end."

I began walking back to my desk, but stopped.

"Oh...is there questions?"

"*Are* there questions?!" Sister Rose Marie hollered out, correcting me.

"Yes, *are* there questions?" I asked.

"Where is the garden?" Cheryl Chan asked.

"In our back yard," I replied.

"How much water do you give the flowers?" Elaine Wong wondered.

"I dunno. We water it about once a week...when my father tells me to."

"Are there any more questions, class?" Sister Rose Marie asked.

"Yeah. Do you have a cow in your garden?" someone yelled out.

"That's enough, Kevin," the Sister warned. "Wasn't that a nice report, class? Let's give him a big hand."

Everyone clapped except Kevin, who booed. It was payback for the hell I put him through during his presentation on farm animals.

The bell that dismissed us finally rang. As I rushed for the door, Sister Rose Marie called out my name.

"William Lee...a minute of your time please," she shouted.

Uh oh, I thought. *Now what.*

"William, that flower you brought in is beautiful," she said. "It looks familiar. Do you know where the plant came from?"

"I dunno," I quickly replied, as I took another step toward the door.

"Perhaps your dad purchased it in a nursery around here. I'd really like to know where I've seen it before. Perhaps I can plant some in our convent."

"I dunno," I repeated.

"Why don't you ask him and let me know," she said.

"Here," I said, extending my hand and offering the crumpled flower. "You can have this one, okay?"

She broke out in laughter as I tried, unsuccessfully, to squirm my way out.

"Let me know tomorrow," she insisted. "That's all for now. You have a nice evening."

Doing a report on the garden was supposed to be a simple assignment. My teacher's recognition of the flower flustered me. There was something embarrassing about our garden. Another shameful secret.

My prayers appeared to have been answered the next day. Sister Rose Marie didn't bring up the subject at all. If pressed, I was prepared to tell her my father received the plant as a gift from a friend, who has since died.

The following Saturday, my father and I were returning home and past the school. As we approached the convent entrance, the door opened and Sister Rose Marie stepped out, carrying a planter box.

"Hello there," she said, startling me as she placed the box down.

My father and I stopped. He associated her with the school but didn't know exactly who she was.

"Chaer hai ngor ga sien shan" (This is my teacher), I whispered.

"Aaah...how ah yue?" my father asked politely.

"You must be Mr. Lee," she said excitedly.

"Yea Siir," he replied, incorrectly."

"I'm glad to finally meet you," she said.

"Thaang yue, veerly nicee," he replied.

"Jhow la" (Let's go), I whispered, sensing trouble.

As my father picked up the signal and stepped away, she motioned to him.

"Oh, by the way, Mr. Lee. The flower your son brought to school from your garden was beautiful," she exclaimed.

"Aaah...veerly beau-tee-fool," he replied.

"I recognized them from somewhere. Would you tell me where I can purchase them?" she asked. "I understand you planted everything yourself."

Suddenly my father became nervous and immediately broke eye contact with her.

"Umm, sor-lee, no Eng-lish," he announced as he quickly scurried away. I was right on his tail. Being rude to my teacher was the last concern I had.

When my father created his garden, his taste was impeccable; his behavior though, was disgraceful. He had no respect or regard for other people's property or feelings.

My father habitually carried a bag and spoon in his suit pocket. He went around the city, trespassing into people's gardens and uprooting their most beautiful plants; he outright stole them. He came home and meticulously replanted them in the garden.

At times I'd walk home through surrounding neighborhoods and recognize his handiwork—bare spots in gardens along the way. He acted like he was entitled to them, never displaying any remorse. I suspected that Sister Rose Marie may have actually seen that plant before my father did his number on it. I was just waiting for her to put two and two together. Fortunately, she never brought the subject up again. Years later, in therapy, I described my father's back yard as the larceny garden.

Sister Rose Marie was actually my favorite teacher there. When I left Saint Mary's, Sister Mildred bid me good riddance, while Sister Rose Marie presented me with a farewell gift. It was a beautiful wooden box with a crucifix on the lid. The box is still very precious to me. One year later, she gave up her vows and returned to Eureka, California. She was the only teacher at the school who treated me with respect. Even when she disciplined me, it was fair and carried out with dignity.

———————————

Favoritism exists in families. Dorothy was Ah Yeh's favorite; my mother adored James; and I was my father's honorable son. In order to maintain my status as favorite child, I became my father's property manager.

In the beginning, I had to compete against my older siblings for the coveted position. I cleaned, mended, painted, prepared rental listings, screened potential renters, composed and typed lease agreements, and maintained communications with tenants. This provided an opportunity to spend time with my father when he wasn't drunk or gambling. But I got in way over my head with some of the responsibilities.

For a child of nine to stand in small claims court before a judge representing his father against a tenant was terrifying. Being taken out of school seemed fun at first, but once we got to the courthouse, I was scared to death. Waiting for our case to be called was stressful. The judge, who had thin graying hair and a slightly hunched back, never smiled and screamed at everyone.

"Lee versus Hamilton," the clerk announced. "Please step up." After we were sworn in, the judge spoke.

"Proceed, Mr. Lee," the judge instructed.

I began, "My name is William Lee and I am the landlord's son. This is my father. He doesn't speak English very well. I met the tenant before she moved in and spoke to her each time about the rent and other problems."

Going over my chronological notes, I presented our case. It felt like everyone present was staring at me with magnifying glasses.

When I finished, our tenant spoke, a young woman in her early twenties, holding a crying baby with another toddler by her side.

"I informed the landlord's son after I moved in that I lost my job and have no money. I told him I would pay them as soon as I can." That was her only response.

We prevailed in that case. My parents had a big argument the previous night. My father wanted me to lie about what she owed us, disregarding cash payments we received in order to receive a higher judgment. My mother wouldn't allow it. I presented the facts as they were. It didn't matter, she never paid what she owed and we were just glad to be rid of her.

I didn't know what to expect when I stepped into that courtroom. My father was proud of me but it took quite a while for me to recover from that ordeal.

I processed evictions and responded to building inspectors, attorneys and hostile tenants; there was no end to the madness. Screening potential renters was something I was very good at and had a vested interest in. My father made serious mistakes selecting tenants early on, and I inherited his problems.

He rented to one person and suddenly six people were living there. Pets that weren't allowed ran rampant; checks bounced; accounts were closed; all-night parties with blaring music became a ritual; fights broke out and police had to be called.

A couple showed up inquiring about the apartment and impressed my father, but I had bad vibes about them. Perhaps they reminded me of my parents or characters from the streets who didn't respect each other. Against my advice, he rented to them. They split up in the second month and the remaining party couldn't make the rent.

I had a reprieve from managing the property when I was hospitalized in 1965. I was ten and cardiologists at the University of California Medical Center performed an angiogram.

The frightening surgical procedure is still vivid in my mind. I was medicated but kept awake. Earphones were placed over my head and a fairy tale was played. A catheter was inserted into my right arm and routed to my heart through an artery. It felt like a construction crew was tearing into my arm. Blue dye was injected through the tubes and blood flowing in my arteries carefully analyzed. Following surgery, I felt like a freak as the dye passed out in my urine.

In the hospital, I slept in my own bed and that was a treat. It was quiet and I didn't have to worry about violent arguments erupting. Unfortunately, the doctors' findings were inconclusive.

Overall, purchasing the first building proved to be a good investment for my parents. In a relatively short period of time, debts to friends were repaid and the property appreciated substantially in value. When I was twelve, we finally moved into one of the flats.

As I entered middle school, my parents took out a second mortgage and purchased another property. An apartment building in Pacific Heights, it was a brand new structure that the developer placed on the market. I nicknamed it The Lemon. The place seemed jinxed or possessed, perhaps both.

Countless water heaters were replaced; the elevator was always on the blink; plumbing throughout the building leaked; heaters and garbage disposals were faulty.

And the automatic garage door opener constantly jammed two feet from the ground; cars couldn't get in or out. It didn't make any sense—all the appliances were new.

We were frequently awakened in the middle of the night by tenants and had to rush over by bus or cab. I begged my father to sell The Lemon but he was reluctant.

My father enjoyed sitting in Chinatown having coffee with his friends, bragging about how much property they owned and how well-off they were. I called it "Keeping Up with the Wongs." He admitted to hanging on to the second piece of property so he wouldn't *sut mein* (lose face). With his circle of friends, it was always about saving face.

Of course, I'd be sitting there next to him trying to stay awake after being up all night responding to complaints. We hung on to The Lemon for six grueling years.

When I balked at the responsibilities of managing the properties, my father withheld his affection and treated me like an ungrateful son. I constantly reminded him that my older siblings should bear some of the weight, but he said I was the only one he could trust to get things done right. I chastised myself for taking the job in the first place.

I was still in college, living at home when we faced the "tenant from hell." I'm not proud of how I dealt with the problem.

Our garden apartment was vacant and we placed an ad in the paper. Several parties inquired, and a fella who stopped by impressed my father. I met him that evening in our living room.

"Hi, Mr. Beaumont?" I asked.

"Yes, you must be Mr. Lee's son," he replied. "Nice to meet you."

Beaumont was just over six-feet, overweight, with an annoying smirk on his face. He reminded me of a young Captain Kangaroo.

"I understand you just moved here," I said.

"That's right," he replied. "My company is opening a store here and wanted me to get things set up. I've been with them three years. I told your father my accounts are being transferred out here and I should be able to give him a check this week. I have the first month's rent with me in cash. Here, Mr. Lee," he said, placing a wad of twenty dollar bills in front of my father.

"*Um ho law ah*" (Don't take it), I instructed my father. But the sight of cash distorted my father's better judgment and he grabbed it.

"Your garden is so beautiful, Mr. Lee," the prospective tenant said as my father began counting the money.

I didn't trust the guy. He was pretentious and smooth, and kept dodging my questions. He said what my father wanted to hear. He portrayed himself as quiet, someone who didn't care for loud music or parties. My father and I spoke in the kitchen. I proposed holding off until we checked his references in Chicago. I also wanted to wait until he remitted the balance of the last month's rent and security deposit.

My father was already mesmerized by the man and the cash he dangled. Before I knew it, my father handed over the keys and encouraged Beaumont to move in immediately. We argued that night about his decision. My father cut me off and assured me that his ability to read people was above reproach. The truth is that his track record was horrible.

We never received another cent from Mr. Beaumont. He wasn't employed and had been living in the city for quite some time. After moving in, he partied every night, disturbing the other tenants and physically threatening them when they complained.

The guy was running a scam. He was fully aware of his rights and the timeframe required to have the sheriff evict him. We were told that when my father gave him the keys and allowed him to move in, it constituted a landlord-tenant relationship.

Our main concern was the damage he may cause to our property, not to mention the disruption to our other tenants. My father repeated over and over that he should have listened to me, but what's done was done. We had a serious problem at hand. My mother was worried that if we threatened or upset Mr. Beaumont, that he'd burn the place down.

As we were processing the eviction, he threw a wild party one evening and the police had to be called. The next day, I ran into him and he was quite belligerent.

"Did you call the police on me?!" he shouted.

"What's your problem?" I asked.

"Fuck, *I'm* your problem!" he shouted. "If you and your father aren't careful, I'm going to tear the place apart. You think you can kick me out that easily. I'm going to be here a while...and there's nothin' you can do about it."

He was wrong. That evening, I came home and my mother was ecstatic.

"Chaer boon gun ah...Chaer boon gun ah!" (He's moving out...He's moving out!)

"Chaer hai?" (He is?) I replied, pretending to be surprised.

He vacated the apartment in less than two hours. My father was quite pleased; everyone in the building celebrated.

Sad but true, there are people who don't respond to reason. They interpret common courtesy as a sign of weakness. The way Beaumont was dealt with was simple. I had some friends pay him a visit earlier in the day. They didn't lay a hand on him. He was given twenty-four hours to clear out. He was told if there was any damage, it'd be taken out of his "hide." He cried like a baby, begging that his life be spared.

My parents never knew why he left in such a hurry.

Beaumont functioned on the dark side. He found out the hard way that my world was even darker. Contrary to stereotypes about Chinese people, quite a number of us are not meek, passive, law-abiding citizens. Being a street punk was what I knew.

CHAPTER 4.

HOCK SAIR WOEY, THE CHINESE UNDERWORLD

I was eight when I witnessed my first shooting. There had been an ongoing feud between Chinese kids and *Bloods* (Blacks) from nearby Telegraph Hill. It was the Fourth of July weekend, a street carnival was operating on Waverly Place in Chinatown, and a "rumble" was declared for ten p.m. My father was out gambling while my mother was putting in a fourteen-hour shift at the garment factory. Kids at Chinese Playground had been whispering about the showdown all day long. I thought to myself, *Nothin's gonna stop me from being there.*

At nine thirty p.m., my friends and me, pint-sized little rascals, were walking around and keeping an eye out for any Bloods as well as the police. Guys from opposing sides showed up around nine forty-five p.m. The groups, each numbering close to forty, gathered and faced each other at the south end of the alley near the ferris wheel. Not a single cop was in sight. Clubs, pipes and chains were brought out, as well as rumble belts and butterfly and switchblade knives. I was in the neutral zone with the Bloods to my left and our guys on the right.

"WHAT THE FUCK YOU LOOKING AT?" someone yelled.

As they began charging one another, I heard someone scream, "NO!" To my right, two Chinese dudes facing one another appeared to be grappling with something. Suddenly there was a loud BANG!

I thought it was a firecracker. There was a puff of smoke and I saw one of the guys keeling over.

"GUN!" a dude screamed.

As people scattered in different directions, I was shoved from side to side. Just as I began to run, someone clipped my shoe, causing me to fall. Two older kids I recognized from the playground tumbled over me. Diving into a narrow doorway, I pushed the heel of my foot back into my tennis shoe and dashed back out. I ran straight home. Entering the apartment, I didn't dare look at my mother for fear she would see right through me.

Back then, guns were unheard of in Chinatown. I couldn't sleep that night. Pop! Pop! Pop! kept going off in my head. *Don't be afraid...that's for chumps,* I told myself.

At the playground the following day, one of the older guys said, "Yea, John's brother tried to stop him from shooting the *Hock Gwais* (Black Devils) and he accidentally shot him. He's in the hospital and John got busted."

"Yea, I was there, man, and it was really cool," I said. I already knew how to act like a big shot to gain respect.

The Chinese gangs I recall from the late 1950s to early '60s included groups such as the Fong-Fong Boys, Raiders, Phoenician Warriors, Majestics, Immortals and Black Bugs. Fong-Fong was a cafe on Stockton Street and a hang-out for kids who naturally adopted the name. My uncle Johnny was a waiter there.

Mary, my oldest sister, headed up her own girl's gang while James "hanged" with the Black Bugs. His initiation late one night at Portsmouth Square bordering Chinatown was interrupted by the police and his boys ran out on him. The behavior of his pals taught me that, out on the streets, it was every man for himself.

Gang activity was typical. The "Tel-Hi" Blacks and white kids who came into our area were regarded as intruders and subject to attack. Clashes also occurred among the Chinese factions but it was just over adolescent stuff like girls, gossip and hard looks. Crime was basically limited to assaults, shoplifting, burglaries and auto theft. Dances were held at Victory Hall on Stockton Street and the YMCA on Clay Street. Kids danced to the tunes of Smokey Robinson and the Miracles, Martha Reeves & the Vandellas, the Shirelles and the Temptations. We hated the Hock Gwais (Black Devils), but we were enamored with their "soul" music and rhythm. Despising them while at the same time admiring their culture didn't make sense to me.

Beginning in 1962, we experienced an influx of families from the Hong Kong region. At that time, The Raiders, Jr. Raiders and even Baby Raiders (junior-high school age) ruled the neighborhood.

Chinese was my first language so it was easy making friends with the newcomers. Back then, my family was still struggling with assimilating into the culture here. We had a lot in common with the recent immigrants.

At schools, especially Galileo High and Marina Middle School, fights were breaking out among the *ABCs* (American-born Chinese) and *FOBs* (foreign-born Chinese). It began with the newcomers getting hassled.

"Fresh-Off-The-Boat!"

"Fuckin' China Bugs!"

"Ching Chongs!"

"Look at them clothes, dude!"

"No speaka' English?"

Even back then, if you didn't wear the right shoes, like Converse, you weren't shit. The native kids, in turn, were called *Jook Sings* (half-devils) and *Tow Gee* (privileged and spoiled landowners). As the conflict escalated, I found myself caught in the middle, technically an ABC, yet identifying with the foreign-borns.

In 1964, a group of immigrant kids got together and formed the Wah Ching (Chinese Youth) gang. They started with only a dozen but their membership grew rapidly. It was payback time and their retaliation was fierce.

This was now a different ball game. ABCs were getting jumped left and right and the beatings were severe. After school, if you made it out of the grounds, they'd find you at the bus stop or cable car turn-table. It wasn't just a one-time payback. The assaults were repeated over and over. Make fun of any foreign-born kid in class or bump one of their brothers or cousins in the hall and you'd pay dearly for it. These guys grew up on the rough streets of Hong Kong and Macao where gangs were hardcore. Many had spent a good part of their youths in brutal prisons.

This was now *their* Chinatown. I spoke their language and never ridiculed them. Although they never came after me, I knew I wasn't impervious to their reign of terror. Yet it also came down to what was seen in the locker room. Essentially, the ABCs were circumcised and the FOBs were not. Ridiculous as it seemed, one's foreskin, or lack of, determined their fate.

My friend, Thomas, spoke fluent English and I assumed he was an ABC until I saw him in the shower. Later, I learned his family emigrated here when he was an infant. It didn't make any difference to me, but one day, he offended one of the foreign-born kids and they were ready to pounce on another ABC. When word got out that Thomas was not circumcised, the FOBs realized he was one of their own, and they spared him.

The Wah Chings hung out at Chinese Playground, and their first clubhouse was on Clay Street across from Portsmouth Square. I generally stayed out of their way. If you were playing basketball, ping-pong or volleyball, and they approached, common sense dictated that you step aside. I got to know a few of them, and on occasion, they invited me to join in. By '69, numerous gangs were formed from the original Wah Chings.

At first, I found it exciting to know some of the gang members. In time, it became clear that they couldn't be trusted. They had ulterior motives. When they were friendly toward me, there was a catch.

"Hold this for me."

"Give so and so a message."

"Hide this for me."

"When the police come, say this..."

"Don't tell anyone you saw this."

I came to believe that everyone was a user and your friends can betray you. There were times I felt I couldn't take it anymore. There were so many things hidden at home, and now, the streets and playground were filled with "hush-hush" and seedy characters.

My passion for *kung-fu* movies brought me to the cinema on a weekly basis. The Great Star, Sun Sing, Grandview, World and Palace Theaters were Chinatown landmarks. I couldn't wait for the new Shaw Brothers and Golden Harvest "flicks" to arrive.

"The One-Armed Swordsman," "Boxer From Shantung" and the "Shaolin Temple" series were classics. The genre had an interesting theme. The heroes were Robin Hood-types defending the common people against corrupt, oppressive officials and their imperial forces. Crimes committed by the rebels were somehow justified.

Brotherhood, courage and loyalty prevailed over oppression, greed and betrayals, with revenge thrown in for action.

These movie houses were also where gang members gathered and established their turf. At times, there was more violence *in* the theater than on the screen.

One Sunday afternoon, inside Sun Sing theater, a man and his girlfriend were seated near the screen. I was about three rows behind them. Suddenly, about fifteen gang members entered. They marched past me and approached the couple. Through the darkness, their shadows and movements were frightening. I knew they were on a violent mission.

"Let's talk outside...everything's okay," one of them said.

The man whispered something to his girlfriend. He then stood up and walked out with them. I sat there and began counting in my head—one thousand one...one thousand two...one thousand three...anticipating the outcome.

As they were leading the man up the aisle, surrounding him on all sides, he was jumped. I knew the routine, so I tried to keep my eyes locked on the screen. It lasted no more than fifteen seconds, but it was horrific. The attack was much worst than others I had witnessed.

"Oh my God! Somebody please help him!" his girlfriend screamed, as she ran to him. I wanted to stop her for her own safety, but I knew better than to get involved.

After the assailants left, I walked over and saw the victim on the ground, badly beaten and bloodied. A number of them had bottles and smashed the man with them. His face was slashed, up and down and side to side, from the broken glass.

"Honey, don't move," she cried. "Shit, look what they did to him."

Finally he was helped out of the theater. The lights never came on and the police never showed up. While most of the patrons left, I slowly returned to my seat and just sat there. My heart was racing but the rest of my body felt numb.

I was curious as to why so many of them attacked him. They were pushing one another aside to get in on it, as though they were competing.

I was twelve at the time. For weeks, I couldn't shake the image of the man's bloodied face. The loud, stomping sound of his beating and his cries for mercy also played over and over again.

As each day passed, the violence became increasingly brutal. I remember feeling like a "fraidy cat," and told myself that I had to get used to all the shit that goes down on the streets. This was my home.

At the playground, gang members shared stories of "jobs" they were hired for, which included the beating of people and robbing of patrons as they left gambling dens. Various *Tongs* ran the games and kids were paid as "look-sees," signaling when police or trouble loomed. (The word "Tong" translates to a meeting hall or club in Chinese. "Hock Sair Woey" which means black society, encompasses the entire Chinese Underworld, including Tongs, Triads and organized street gangs. In the Orient today, one particular Triad has a reported membership of more than 50,000. It is my belief that the Hock Sair Woey embodies the most powerful criminal element in the world.)

Once, someone powerful in Chinatown wanted a man beaten up. They located him in a movie house. Unbeknownst to them, their victim, about sixty years old, was a skilled martial artist. It began with eight of them surrounding the man.

As one of the gang members recalled, "I've never seen anyone fight like that. The old man was actually beating the shit out of us. Luckily, someone ran out, got more guys, and we were able to crowd and put him down. We ended up knocking out most of his teeth, man!"

As he shared the story, I found myself rooting for the old guy. The ending stunk as I saw the victim as a fallen kung-fu hero. But I just sat there and laughed along, pretending to be amused. The fact that these guys were hired meant that the Tongs were stepping out after years of obscurity.

I grew up hearing about the infamous Tong Wars with Little Pete and the "hatchet men." Tales of prostitution, opium dens, gambling halls and secret passages running through Chinatown were legendary. As a young boy, I was told by older kids that these groups protected early Chinese settlers against abuses of the white men, but they were also involved in criminal activities. Various Tongs engaged in battle to control the neighborhood rackets.

As kids, we role-played in the same alleys where the bloody confrontations took place. Chasing one another, with knives tucked in our sleeves, we screamed, "You dare mess with my Tong! Where's my money? You die, ass-hole!"

For kicks, we tip-toed up to the Hop Sing Tong headquarters. I knocked on the door and ran away, yelling, "*Bui how doi* [hatchet man] is chasing me!"

The major West Coast Tongs were the *Bing Kung, Hop Sing, Hip Sing and Suey Sing.* My Uncle Wong (Yin Doon), who was personal friends with Chiang Kai Shek, headed the powerful Bing Kung Tong. He also led the Wong Family Association and was the top member of the Republic of China's Kuomintang Nationalist Party in the U.S.

As far back as I can remember, the KMT has always been regarded as the controlling force of *Jhong Wah Wuey Goon* (the Chinese Six Companies). Virtually all Tong elders were members of the KMT.

Wong Yin Doon took my father under his wings in the early 1960s, and I was told to, *joon ging* (respect) him. No problem—to me, Wong Bok Bok (Uncle Wong) was my sparring partner. I usually greeted him by running up and we would then get in our fighting stance. I declared, *"Ngor hai Wong Fay Hung!"* (I am the kung-fu hero!) then punched him.

Leaders of the other Tongs were close to my father as well, but I didn't associate them or my father with gangs. To me, they were just mild-mannered men that we had lunch and coffee with. The Tong leaders, as well as my father, walked through Chinatown hunched slightly forward with their hands clasped behind their backs. Their tailored suits with fancy tie clips and jade rings distinguished them from the common man. And like my father and Wong Bok Bok, some of them wore a gold lapel pin with a miniature photo of Sun Yat Sen. They didn't appear ruthless to me. Actually, I thought they were boring.

Chinese men are hospitable and fight over restaurant checks. I sat and analyzed the ritual. Individuals such as my father and Wong Bok Bok were sincere in grabbing the checks. But there were a few who stuck their arms out and only made phony attempts to grab the bill from the waiters and waitresses. In my eyes, a full-arm's length grab was sincere; half-length was "chicken shit." The stingy ones were actually the wealthiest in the group, with large property holdings in Chinatown. I kept encouraging my father to call them on it. There were times I felt like yelling, "Hey, you guys should pay since you never do...you're *goo horn!*" (stingy!)

They watched over me but I considered them nosy spies reporting my activities back to my father. Years later, it would be noted by writers, journalists and historians that Wong Bok Bok was indisputably *the* most powerful Chinese in America during his time.

I have very fond memories of my time at Marina Middle School. The halls were immaculately clean and the cafeteria offered great food. I can still smell the giant peanut-butter cookies that were ten cents each. We hung out, got in fights, played ball, listened to music, teased girls, snuck peeks at Playboy centerfolds...that was the life.

Along with my friends, we ruled the school. Once, ten of us had a plan to leave school early and brought notes forged with our parents' signatures. Around nine a.m., Mr. Wong, the Dean of Boys (whom we accused of being a racist "banana"—yellow on the outside; white on the inside), summoned us to his office.

"You boys are in trouble and I've got you this time," he shouted. "I have in front of me, your notes *and* your emergency contact cards which were turned in at the beginning of the school year. Now, one by one, I'm going to compare the signatures. I bet they're not going to match. Gentlemen, all of you are looking at detention."

He went through the process, one by one, confirming his hunch.

"Daniel Jeung...detention!"

"Ernest Yee...detention!"

"Calvin Wong...detention!"

"Victor Seto...detention!"

Eventually, he reached my note and card. I sat there with a smirk on my face.

"William Lee...dee...hmm..."

He was stunned. "It matches!" he whispered. "Okay, I guess you're excused to leave, Mr. Lee."

Later, my friends all wondered how my note and emergency card matched. "Oh, that's simple," I explained. "I've been forging my parents' signature on everything from the school."

Everyone thought that was so cool, but it was quite pathetic. My father and mother were always too busy to care what was going on at school, so I signed all the documents.

Many of my childhood friends became criminals who made front-page news. Walter Teng, from my Marina days, was among them.

One of the foreign-born kids I got along well with, Walter shared a number of classes with me. He was quite big and tough. Walter was quiet, yet always ready to step in when I needed some muscle. I think he was amused at what a "loud-mouth" I was.

I wondered which gang he would end up with. Walter didn't get drawn into the gang wars, but he was convicted as one of the "Ski Mask Bandits" who were linked to eight armed robberies over a two-month period in 1973, which included two banks, before they were apprehended. I never saw Walter again and worried that he died in prison or at the hands of his parents.

I was all of 4'6" in seventh grade but that didn't stop me from bullying a lot of the big kids. My "patsies" were required to bring me candy at school on a daily basis. Those who didn't comply received "knuckle sandwiches." I never stopped to consider the feelings of the people I tormented. In my mind it was justified, since I was being picked on by older thugs.

Stanley Varner was a sweet, smart kid that I harassed for two years in middle school. Every opportunity I had, I made fun of him and pushed him around. One day, he confronted me before class started.

"You have been making my life miserable!" he shouted.

"My psychologist tells me I am not responsible for your abusive childhood.

I don't care what you do to me, but this has got to stop!"

I watched as his face quickly turned bright red and tears filled his glasses. He really caught me off guard, especially his statement about the psychologist. I didn't realize I had driven him to counseling and they were talking about me.

My first reaction was to punch him, but as our classmates began entering the room. I simply whispered, "Okay, man...cool it."

Stanley and I attended Galileo High School together and he served in many offices, including class president. I stayed away from him to honor my word but also because he intimidated me. I was afraid he and his therapist had me all figured out.

1970 was the year my friends and I tangled with the underworld gangs. My best friends were Daniel, Cal and Vic. We trained together at a kung-fu studio and were regarded as the top four students. Our *Sifu* (Master) taught us full-contact sparring and street-fighting. We didn't wear protective gear in those days. Just a lot of bruises that Sifu treated with smelly ointment. We thought we were bad asses, always looking for an excuse to fight. Of course, it was only a matter of time before we messed with the wrong people.

During Chinese New Year's, there was intense competition among the kung-fu clubs to perform Lion Dancing for businesses and groups in Chinatown. Firecrackers were used to scare away the evil spirits, but we were after the *Lai See* (red envelopes containing money). A lot of cash was at stake and selection for performances was political. Kung-fu studios also served as recruiting grounds for various Tongs. Some of the Sifus were Tong enforcers.

One particular Saturday, we were coordinating the work and proceeds with another studio. Eight of us were crammed in the back of a truck with a huge drum, cymbals, lion-head and other equipment cruising through Chinatown.

This kid named Johnny from the other studio and I were in each other's faces from the start over who played the drum. A bit taller than me but thinner, I could tell he was raised on the streets in Hong Kong.

The tension was building with dirty looks being exchanged and light shoves to establish rank within the truck. Finally I shouted, "Move over, man, quit hogging the drum." He wouldn't budge so I pushed him aside and took over. I stood ready to fight but he backed away. I figured he was just another punk that needed to be taught a lesson. But this was not the end of it.

A short time later, Johnny clobbered me. He snuck up behind me, wrapped his arm around my neck and beat me repeatedly with a club, yelling *"Dill nay! Dill nay!"* (Fuck You! Fuck You!) Because we were crammed, I wasn't able to push him back. Unintentionally, my arms were pinned by others attempting to separate us.

Johnny got in at least five good blows. I was a bloody mess. My nose was broken and I started to black out. Blood was gushing everywhere and my eyes were teary. I couldn't believe what had happened. It was obvious I needed medical attention, but we were stuck in traffic.

I remember Cal helping me out of the truck. A hospital was close by, but I refused to go. I was embarrassed and just wanted to hide. Cal assisted me back to our studio.

I looked in the mirror and didn't recognize myself. There were bumps the size of golf balls along my forehead. The bridge of my nose had swelled up and was crackling. My clothes were soaked in blood, which continued pouring out. I thought I was going to bleed to death. Cal left to find Sifu.

Finally, the bleeding stopped. At that point, I just wanted to put a bag over my head and run home, but my intuition told me something bad was goin' down.

I located my group a few blocks away on Grant Avenue. Cal was already there so my classmates knew what had happened. Johnny and his group were just ahead. Sifu was already heading toward them. "Sifu," I yelled. He walked over to me and had a crazed look in his eyes.

"Look at you!" he screamed. "That guy's going to pay for this. And if anyone gets in the way, I'm kicking their ass, too!"

He moved in their direction as my classmates, nearly twenty of them, were prepared to attack the other members as well. I thought to myself, *Shit, someone's going to get killed...I have to do something.*

"Sifu, please don't," I pleaded. "I don't want anyone else to get hurt." I don't know how, but I restrained him and our group eventually calmed down.

When I arrived home, my mother had already heard. She knew I wasn't an angel and got into scrapes, but the way I was beaten didn't sit well with her.

"Your father called...he's on his way," she said.

I couldn't wait for my father to get home, but I was also terrified that he'd be upset at me. When he arrived, he didn't say much. While he was treating my injuries, I noticed his hands trembling and his jaw muscles pulsating in anger. He was continually on and off the phone.

Finally, he turned to me and said, *"He's a member of Suey Sing Tong."*

My father went on to say that the Tong's president called, concerned about me, expressing sorrow over the attack. Johnny was ordered to appear before my father the next day.

My father whispered, *"This is a courtesy from them. Under normal circumstances, they would back the punk up because he's their people. How would it look to the other gang members if the elders did not support them. It's important that you understand this about the Tongs."*

I understood what he was saying but I was consumed with guilt and fear. Because of me, my father was suddenly going up against a powerful Tong.

The following day, I intercepted the meeting between Johnny and my father. I had no desire to leave the house looking like hell, but I had to do something. I met up with Johnny on Jackson Street in front of the Suey Sing Tong headquarters.

"I sorry man," he said. "I go crazy afta' you push me."

"Let's try to forget it," I replied.

"I go see your fatha' now. You know what he wanna do?"

"Well, I'll go talk to him. You don't have to see him."

"You sure?" he asked. "I know I sapposed to see him."

"Yea, I'll take care of it."

"Okay, I see you 'round then, he said." We shook hands and parted ways.

My father wasn't thrilled when I went to see him in Johnny's place. He was upset with me, but I couldn't afford to second-guess my father, the Suey Sing Tong, Johnny or anyone else. I was worried that my father may get himself killed because of me. As far as I'm concerned, Chinese are the worst people to cross, holding grudges for decades, until the opportunity for redemption presents itself. Vengeance to restore honor are passed through generations.

I wanted to put this episode behind me, but the beating affected me traumatically. Months after my wounds healed, I was still fearful of getting punched. I refused to spar during kung-fu practice.

Then I realized that the incident hardened me, and my perception of fighting took on a whole new meaning. Scuffles were no longer simply black eyes and bloody noses, ending when someone got pinned or declared, "I give up." I started to believe that Johnny could have killed me.

As time passed, my propensity for violence increased. I was constantly on edge. My paranoia was now drawing out the brutal side of me. I knew that if provoked, I could really hurt someone for fear of my life. I wasn't going to ever let anyone get the upper hand on me again.

One of my classmates, Raymond, also had a run-in with a gang member around the same time. Raymond's father, Mr. Chong, had gone to the Palace Theater one Saturday afternoon. After entering, he realized he needed to return home. Mr. Chong asked the ticket collector for permission to step out and come back in. *"Haer la"* (Go ahead), the man replied.

When Raymond's father returned a short time later, a different person was stationed at the door.

"I don't know what you're talking about," the collector said.

An argument ensued. Mr. Chong went home and informed

Raymond about his mistreatment.

Raymond accompanied his father back to the theater and confronted the man. As they were screaming at one another, the collector pushed Raymond and shouted, *"I'm Wah Ching."* Raymond took a step back and came forward with a front kick, landing smack on the jaw of the gangster. As he fell to the ground, the Wah Ching pulled out a .38 and shot Raymond in the abdomen. Fortunately, Raymond recovered.

When I heard what went down, I was surprised that Raymond reacted the way he did. Prior to joining our club, he'd never been in a fight.

I felt that too many of us were resorting to violence. My idea of being a martial artist was based on my legendary hero, Wong Fay Hung, a humble man who avoided confrontations. Something happened to us? We turned into bullies and aggressors.

The Wah Ching and Suey Sing Boys were at war for a short period beginning in 1969 to control Chinatown's underworld of gambling, loan-sharking, extortion and politics. Shootings and homicides in Chinatown filled the front pages of newspapers. By early '70, the "SS Boys" relinquished San Francisco and established Oakland as their territory. I was caught up in the drama and found it exciting. I became indifferent to the violence, accepting it as a normal part of life. There were nightmares here and there, but I learned to ignore it like everything else.

By 1970, Joe Fong—whose older brothers were founding

members of the Wah Chings and he, the youngest member in the gang—was already well-known on the streets and by the police. He'd been to our house and was friends with my sister, May. Joe broke away from the gang and became one of the leaders of a new group, *Yow Lay,* which means Good Fortune. In a short time, their membership grew to more than 150 and they were taking over Chinatown.

Joe and Cal were also good friends, and we discussed joining up but decided against it. "Let's just try to stay cool with everyone in Chinatown," I suggested.

Cal felt an allegiance to Joe, but we remained on our own for the time being. Deep down, I think we all knew that with the Hock Sair Woey (Chinese Underworld) sponsoring Yow Lay, that I'd be odd man out. My father was constantly haranguing me to stay out of the gangs and his underworld associates would never allow me to be initiated into Yow Lay. Besides, my mother was constantly reminding me not to be a burden to her. The idea of having to call her from the police station or the image of myself lying dead in the morgue with her standing over me crying were strong deterrents.

Not long after our discussion, Cal and Vic along with a few other friends were jumped by Wah Chings. They were walking down Clay Street and encountered the gang. David, one of the gang members, confronted them and shouted, "What the fuck you doing in Chinatown!" Punches started flying. With my friends considerably outnumbered, they were getting roughed-up.

Suddenly Sifu appeared out of nowhere. He was driving by and noticed his disciples in trouble. He jumped out of his car and into the fracas.

The fighting ended abruptly when one of the gang members began vomiting blood after Sifu collapsed his lung with a punch to the chest. That was the strength of his *chi kung* (internal power). My friends jumped into Sifu's car. They drove off just as additional gang members arrived, armed with guns.

The fight was enough to push Cal, Daniel, Vic and others in our group over to Joe Fong and the Yow Lay. Sifu was being hunted, the studio closed down and I went my own way.

I'd run into them occasionally and they would usually be in a large group with a tough persona, but to me they were still the same guys that I grew up acting silly with. I missed them, but had few regrets. I wasn't interested in being a hardcore gangster. Not yet, anyway.

Cal was implicated in a shooting of Wah Chings in '72 and subsequently convicted. Although a minor at the time of the crime, he was prosecuted as an adult and sentenced to Dalton State Prison. Dalton is where Joe and many of the guys would also serve time.

Although not hooked up with any gang, I was still running around the streets, hanging around pool halls and the Police Athletic League in Chinatown. The PAL was established to keep kids off the streets, but we turned it into a gambling den where gangs heavily recruited. Guys who couldn't get in or afford the fees at regular pool halls ended up at the PAL.

Gambling was out in the open and the popular game was *Sup*

Som Jhern (Thirteen-Card Poker), where a 52-card deck was dealt to four players, who each strategically arranged three hands of poker. The top hand consisted of three cards, followed by two, five-card hands. Junior and high school kids wagered away upwards of one hundred dollars at a time.

Although the facility was run by a sergeant in the San Francisco Police Department, the place was filled with ruffians and most of us carried weapons. I learned how to check people out and establish rank. I got away with staring anyone down except the hardcore gang members.

It wasn't much fun when these guys joined our poker games. Many were sore losers and made up their own rules. A few blatantly took their winnings but refused to fork over losses. When they entered, I looked for a mutual acquaintance in their group. That was the only way we'd have a chance for a fair game. Walking away wasn't an option.

Once, two of them sat in with us. I knew them by reputation only. One was called *Lun Towl* (Dick-Head), by his friends. About eighteen, he was one of the rowdier ones. After playing a hand, he lost twenty dollars to me but wouldn't pay up. I hesitated before speaking. *Hmm, what should I say? Mr. Dick-head, can you please pay me? Or, hey, Dick-head, pay up!*

Finally I just blurted out, "Um, you owe me twenty dollars."

He immediately sat up and said, "Why the fuck should I give you twenty dollars?

You gonna give me a blow-job?"

I kept quiet; didn't dare look at him and just continued playing. *Man, what an ass-hole,* I thought. *How "bad" are you without your boys and that gun...Dick-head! Try anything and I'll cut it off. Then we'll call you "Dick-less!"*

At times, I became disgusted with the place and swore not to return. But I'd be right back the next day. I couldn't figure it out—it wasn't a nurturing environment, but there was also something familiar about the ambiance. The bullies, the gambling, the violence, the code of silence—I had no idea the place had so much in common with my home. Many of us stopped hanging out there when rumors surfaced that the place was "wired" and our conversations were being recorded by the cops. So we took our gaming elsewhere.

Entering my teens, gambling seemed to be the most important thing in my life. Drugs and alcohol never attracted me, but the rush I got from gambling was irresistible. When worries, troubles or disappointments became overwhelming, I wagered to numb my feelings.

Chinese engage in gambling as a way of socializing. Our parents and relatives served as role models, exposing us to *Mah Jong, Pai Gow, Fan Tan* and other games as an appropriate form of recreation.

I grew up with the concept that gambling was macho—risk-taking, competing, drinking, smoking, cussing, and carrying wads of cash—gambling encompassed these things and represented a rite of passage.

Playing cards in all-night laundromats as a teenager, we threatened people and chased them out of the facilities. We blocked people's doorways in order to lay out our cards and bets. We didn't give a damn about anyone else. Try to stop us from being "in action" and you faced a bunch of hostile, violent kids.

At Galileo High School, I was a terror. Unruly, disrespectful and disruptive, I cut classes on a regular basis, which provided a reprieve for my teachers. My first report card reflected this. An "A" in PE, "C" in English (which I attended occasionally and enjoyed), followed by "F's." I was subsequently suspended and faced expulsion for physically threatening two of my teachers.

It was just easier for me to get on their bad side. I was a smart-mouthed punk just waiting for them to say, "That's it, I give up on you." Fortunately for me, the Assistant Principal, Mr. Stanton Tong, didn't play into my hand.

"You have enormous potential, William. If you would just divert your energy in the proper direction, you can have a great future. If we keep you in school, you have to work with me and really make an effort. What do you say?"

"Yeah, alright. Thanks, Mr. Tong," I replied.

I will never forget the second chance he gave me, which kept me in school and probably saved my life. I was not accustomed to anyone believing in me.

In addition to Mr. Tong, my homeroom teacher and a school counselor also vouched for me. I was determined not to let them down. Facing the prospects of being a high-school dropout was not appealing.

With an attitude adjustment, I began earning straight A's. For the first time in my life, I was proud of myself. Of course, I couldn't let friends in on my stellar grades; I had an image on the streets to maintain.

During that period, I was also hanging around the *Dhon* (East) Ping Yuen housing project. Some of the guys who lived there studied *Tong Long* (Praying Mantis) kung-fu with Wong Joc Mun, the Sifu who fought a famous duel against Bruce Lee in the early '60s. Wong Sifu's studio was located on Pacific Avenue and we hung out there as well. Everyone there called me Little Soul Brother. When Wong Sifu wasn't around, we used to turn off the lights and spar in total darkness. We also engaged in full-contact, "tag-team" matches. It was wild.

As I started my junior year at Galileo, a tragic event took place which forced me to examine my life and mortality. A group of my friends from Chinatown had gone camping and deer hunting in the Sierras. It was the third week of September, 1971. They left on Thursday to get a head start on hunting season, which officially opened on Saturday. Among them was my childhood buddy from St. Mary's, Winston Lew, sixteen, and my hero from the streets, Darren Gee, twenty one.

Winston and I met in third grade. He was always quiet and mellow, never hassled anyone. He wasn't your typical street kid or trouble-maker. Through the years, he grew taller, but his looks and mannerisms remained the same. As we entered our teens, I noticed Winston hanging out with older guys in the neighborhood. Most were former gang members who were usually "stoned."

Darren was the guy I wanted for an older brother. He used to lead us into the elevator shafts, back alleys and high rooftops. He asked my sister Dorothy out on a date once and I never forgave her for turning him down. He was an awesome street-fighter, totally fearless. He was one of the few Raiders the Wah Chings respected. Darren was like a super hero to me.

If someone broke into school at night, bypassed the security and switched on all the lights, we knew it was Darren; or if a building was scaled to scribble graffiti, that would be his signature.

Darren never treated us as pesky kids. On the contrary, he was always respectful. My brother never bullied me when Darren was around. Late at night, we huddled around him on the merry-go-round at Chinese Playground. There, in virtual darkness, he told the scariest ghost stories. As reckless as he was, I always felt safe around him.

Darren entered a "black hole" when his buddy was killed while they were "trippin'" together. I don't recall the exact details. Some say his friend got crushed in an elevator shaft and Darren blamed himself. He escaped from the pain and guilt by turning to glue and drugs. When I saw him at the schoolyard sniffing out of a brown bag, I was devastated. My hero had fallen. He asked me to sit with him but I just walked away. He also asked me for money. Everything changed— he was now someone I knew I had to stay away from. Just say, "hey, what's happening" and that's it.

Looking up to someone and seeing them transform and waste away left me feeling confused and empty. *Who can I really rely on in my life?* I wondered. I prayed for Darren, hoping that he'd snap out of his slump.

Randy Yip, whom I didn't know well, was on the hunting trip. They also took along Ralph Gong, 14, younger brother of my friend,

Lincoln. Their final companion was Clifford Young, 21, a fella known to be on the eccentric side. Clifford was often the target of distasteful jokes and pranks. When I heard he was going on the trip, I figured they took him along for amusement.

I was in a pool hall on Saturday afternoon when the news broke. Word spread quickly through the projects that Lincoln's brother had been shot. Everyone else was dead.

"Crazy Clifford ambushed them with a rifle!" someone shouted.

I couldn't believe it. Winston and I spoke right before they left. He was leaning against a parking meter in Chinatown and I was kidding him about the trip.

"You're going to miss school," I said.

"What's school?" he replied, with a grin.

"Come on, man. This isn't like cutting classes at Saint Mary's," I said.

"You're damn right," he snapped. "I don't have to worry about old Sister Mildred."

The story I heard was that Clifford was being teased throughout the ride up to the mountains. Late Friday morning, while they were getting up, Clifford went to the car, came back with a rifle, and without a word, methodically began blasting away at his tormentors.

Three bodies were found at their campsite on a granite ledge above a creek. One was in the creek and the other two were on the bank. Blood was splattered everywhere. After being shot in the chest and left for dead, Ralph crawled two hundred yards to the highway and was spotted by a motorist. He gave a description of their car and within an hour, Clifford was arrested.

Even with Darren struggling with his problems, he was still invincible to me. In my mind, nothing could kill him—not drugs, bullets, steel elevators—nothing. And Winston, I couldn't stop thinking about our early days in grammar school together. He will always be remembered as the sweet, quiet kid I knew.

Four hunting rifles were found. Even as the Justice of the Peace issued a gag order, the news reported that a drug search was conducted at the campsite. The following year, Clifford was convicted for the murders and committed to a mental institution.

About eighteen months later, the son-of-a-bitch strolled into Mike's Pool Hall on a day outing with his fellow patients. When I saw him, I didn't know whether I should attack him or run away. You better believe I kept a close eye on him. People like that were unpredictable. They were liable to "go off" at any time.

It was easier to deal with people getting shot and killed in the neighborhood if you only knew them casually or if they were in a gang. Darren and Winston's death was totally unexpected and I didn't know how to deal with it. I never told anyone how confused I was. *Is this God's way of putting them out of their misery? Will he be coming after me soon? Do the good really die young, or does he take punks like me first?*

After Cal and the guys joined up with Joe Fong, my best friend was Trent Yee. We hung around the projects, sold fireworks, got into fights, played basketball, shot pool and gambled together. On the streets, it was imperative to have a partner— someone you can count on, above and beyond your own family. You watched each other's back, no matter what.

Trent was very bright, possessed street-smarts and had guts. Various gangs tried to recruit him. He was continually invited to party with the big boys.

"Stay away from them, dude," I said.

"Don't worry, man," he replied. "I'm not stupid. I don't want to get "popped" or sent away."

"Yea, Trent, we're partners, so don't fuck up!"

Trent began dating a girl who had mutual friends with Joe Fong. These guys had cars, went to nightclubs and dances, and basically turned him on to an exciting lifestyle.

Before I knew it, Trent became a gang member. I continually telephoned him, stopping by his house, but his response was always, "The guys are picking me up." I was invited along but usually declined. I appreciated his courtesy to include me but he was choosing their friendship over mine and I was hurt. Feeling rejected, I was also convinced I was cursed. My best friends were all ending up in gangs.

All things considered, Trent was lucky. Eventually, he was arrested along with about a dozen others during a brawl with Wah Chings, and that was the only trouble he got into.

Jason Fung and Frank Lau, my original buddies from Saint Mary's, were also running around with the wrong people. Frank was busted for committing home burglaries and was sent to a juvenile detention center. Jason got hooked up with a gang and they were robbing grocery stores. During one of their jobs, a grocer was shot and killed. Jason was apprehended and convicted of murder. Prosecuted as an adult, he received a life sentence.

I can still visualize the three of us sitting on the playground steps. We vowed to stay friends forever. They were good guys. We just wanted to survive our homes and the streets. It's sad how things turned out.

CHAPTER 5.
DOIN' THE NINE-BALL HUSTLE

In North Beach, there were two pool halls a block apart, Mike's and Babe's. Both were old-time Italian hang-outs in a neighborhood that was undergoing a transformation due to the migration of people from Chinatown. By 1970, ninety percent of the clientele at both establishments was Chinese, with more foreign-born dudes at Babe's.

Mike's had a dark reputation. It was where some of the toughest guys gathered. You could get your ass kicked just for assuming you're "bad" enough to walk in. It represented a turf claimed by certain elements, just like the playground. You generally didn't mess with anyone who was a regular there. Just being a hard guy wasn't enough to cut it. You had to attain an informal rank on the streets to be allowed. And to be respected for your billiard skills was even more difficult.

A number of my sisters' friends were regulars, and I finagled an invitation to join them for a game of Eight-Ball. I was awestruck when I walked in. Surprisingly, the place was clean and well-maintained. A whiff of disinfectant from the rest room in the rear tickled my sinuses. The proprietor ran the business from behind a long counter, with pinball machines and a jukebox to the right. Three rolls of pool tables were perfectly lined across the hall. Dark burgundy carpeting contrasted with the green felt on each table, which were illuminated by individual hanging lamps.

From that day on, I spent all my spare time there. Mike, a burly Italian who constantly bragged about his grandchildren, owned the place with his son, his namesake. Both spoke kindly of their wives and children but we never saw them. I presumed they didn't want their families anywhere near us.

Most days, I was a truant from school. You'd find me walking in at one p.m. sharp, the earliest minors were allowed. I worked out a deal with Mike, Sr., to brush the tables and place the cue sticks back on the racks in exchange for playing time. The chores made me feel important in the place.

Within those walls, drugs were sold and crimes were conceived. Some guys even tried to rip Mike off by tampering with his pinball machines. The Triple-Play "bagger" games took in a lot of money. If you successfully lined up three, four, or five numbers in straight or diagonal formations, you accumulated points which the "house" paid out in cash. "Cheats" attempted to use magnets, remove the glass, rig the counter or outright steal the coins by breaking or picking the locks.

Valiums, Quaaludes, "weed" and "uppers" were everywhere. Angel Dust (PCP) made its way to the pool hall. Angry young men became monsters. A guy I know was found hanging from his sixth floor window sill. Most turned violent with newfound physical strength. They didn't seem to feel any pain.

Guys who were normally cordial to me acted like monsters under the influence. Most dudes in there were unpredictable to begin with. The "dopers" were just a wee bit more challenging to be around.

Next door to Mike's was Caesar's Latin Night Club. Dark men with slick black hair, shiny shoes and wide lapel jackets escorted beautiful women with stiff, high hairdos and bright, pretty dresses down the stairs, where they danced the night away. Live bands shook the ceiling with crisp, Salsa music. I wanted to sneak down and watch them twist and jiggle. Couples came out looking exhausted, but exuberant.

Late one night, a huge fight broke out in the street between guys from Mike's, who were high, and patrons from Caesar's, who were drunk. Soon everyone got into it. By the time it ended, a man from the night club lay dead on the street.

When I heard about it later in the morning, I rushed over to check out the scene. Broken cue sticks were still rolling along the curb and in the gutter, while broken beer bottles covered areas of the sidewalk and street. Both businesses shut down for about a week.

Part of me regretted missing the action, but I also knew it was a senseless, altercation involving macho guys from both sides stoned out of their minds. If present, I would have been pressured to participate in order to save face and not be labeled a wimp.

By sixteen, I had become one of the top Nine-Ball hustlers there. My ability to position one shot to the next, "shaping the table," was an inherent gift. The skill to con my opponents, though, was learned.

The front table was reserved for the top players and big money games. I walked in one day and a new face was at the "show" table. Handsome, with his hair in a pompadour and a diamond ring on his pinkie finger, the dress shirt he wore was perfectly pressed with sharp creases. He had amazing style and accuracy.

"Mike, who is that?" I asked.

"'King Lum.' Used to be a regular in here before your time. One of the best hustlers in the city...got drafted...just returned from Nam."

I was dazzled by him. Other regulars came in and were very respectful toward him.

The following afternoon, he was back at the same spot, shooting alone. I began playing on the next table. No one else was present. He glanced over at me, repeatedly. I knew he was studying my shots: examining my grip; staring at my alignment and preparation, from the base of the stick.

"Hey kid, you wanna shoot a coupla games?" There was momentary silence.

"Just for fun, right?" I asked.

"For fun? Sure...why not," he replied, with a big grin.

Within a week, he took me on as his protégé. He sharpened my skills, but the bulk of the lessons involved fine-tuning the hustling game. Playing your "mark." Camouflaging your skills and baiting the opponent.

King Lum encouraged me to exploit my youth to receive "spots" or handicaps from older players. Day and night, for months, he passed on his skill and knowledge. If I was intent on being a top hustler, certain values and principles had to be adopted.

He'd say, "There are no rules, limits or compromises, kid. The only code you follow is to look out for yourself. Everyone is a potential target. No one is excluded. If you can hustle your best friend, do it! No mercy. You take every dollar you can and let them cry all the way home."

We traveled to other pool halls and he pointed out players to me who brought out their "cream of the crop" Zimmerman cuesticks, only after the big wager was made. Endless scenarios were detailed to serve as warnings. *There are "ring" games where partners will pretend to be strangers and set one another up for winning shots against their victim(s). Notice the technique change after the hustle is made. Look past their eyes to read their soul. Follow your gut and learn to smell the hustle.*

When a player whips out a Zimmerman cue stick in the middle of the game, you've been had.

The ultimate test was to walk into an unfamiliar pool hall and get into a money game. The "kicker" is that you don't have any cash in your pockets. So, essentially, you're playing for your life. If you can handle that kind of pressure, everything else is "gravy."

When my time came, I walked into Palace Billiards on Market Street. After climbing up the stairs, I found myself inside the biggest parlor in the city. I'd never seen so many pool tables together in my life. The place was crowded and filled with cigarette smoke rising to the ceiling. I inched my way over to the counter unnoticed.

I brought along my cuestick in a vinyl pouch, and in my pocket was a butterfly knife with a four-inch blade which I carried everywhere since age ten. After sitting a bit, I approached the man behind the cash register.

"I'm looking for a game. Nine-Ball for ten."

"Okay," he said.

Within thirty minutes, I was in a game with a fellow named Jake, about twenty, who didn't talk much. He was tall, lanky, had long brown hair and a rough complexion. Fresh acne on his cheeks covered deep-pitted chicken pox scars.

We were assigned a table in the middle of the hall. I was hoping to be as close to the door as possible in case I had to make a run for it.

I fought to stay calm the entire time. I was arguing with myself. *Forget this whole thing and get outta here before it's too late. Call a friend to bring you some money. Pretend you're sick and leave.*

But I knew if I ever wanted to walk back into Mike's and hold my head up, this had to be done. My heart was pounding and my eyelids were twitching uncontrollably. I went to the bathroom, looked in the mirror and was pale as a ghost. *This is it, baby!*

In those days, you didn't ask to see the money or deposit it with a neutral person. It wasn't an honor system. People just knew better than to rip someone off.

We're not dealing with characters who accepted being played for a stooge and letting you walk away.

Under normal circumstances, I'd "tank" or purposely lose to set up my mark for bigger stakes. But of course my objective wasn't to hustle anyone that day. I just wanted to get out of there in one piece.

We started off playing straight-up with neither one of us getting a handicap. I won the first game after he missed the seven ball. I knocked in the seven, then the eight and finally the money nine-ball in one sequence. I went on to win the second game. At that point, I was ahead twenty dollars.

"How about the next game for twenty?" he asked.

"No, not yet," I replied.

I may not have been working a hustle, but he was. After realizing I wouldn't budge on the stakes and that we might never see each other again, his hidden skills were displayed and he won the next two games.

Back to square one. We were dead even, but I didn't have any money for the table fee.

"How about one more game for twenty?" Jake proposed.

"No, you're too good for me," I replied, shaking my head.

"Aw, come on, I think you're better," he said.

I started unscrewing my cuestick and waited for him to offer a "spot."

"Alright," he said. "I'll give you eight safe." (That meant if I hit the eight-ball in, it protects me from losing the game.)

I wanted to squeeze him a little more. Jake was hooked and needed to be in action.

"I need eight good," I insisted. (That gave me two chances. I'd win by hitting in either the eight or nine balls.)

No response—by now, my stick was completely in the case and I was reaching for my jacket. I was excited about "reeling in my fish."

"Man...yeah, let's do it," he said reluctantly.

"Twenty and the table time, too. Right, Jake?"

"Fine."

It was a quick game. I took my time lining up each shot, analyzing the position of each ball. I chalked up after each shot and hit the eight ball in after he missed a combination shot. I took my twenty dollars and started to leave.

"So where do you shoot at?" he asked.

"Mike's. Just ask for Little Soul Brother," I replied.

I strutted out of there like I had just achieved my manhood. I returned to Mike's and bragged all night long.

One day, a husky Caucasian fella with long blonde hair entered

Mike's wearing overalls and carrying his stick in a square black case. He looked like a farmer. He wanted to play Nine-Ball for money, and one of the guys obliged. When it came time to pay up, he didn't have any money. He was dragged out onto the street and worked over pretty good. They took his stick and called the police. He wasn't very skilled so I don't think he was in there to prove anything. He was just stupid.

A fella named Philly also taught me a great deal about hustling. He was Eurasian, in his forties, quiet, with dark complexion and heavy bags under his eyes. I heard he was supposedly on the run, hiding out in the city. Rumor had it that he was a hit man for the mob in Chicago. He smoked Sherman cigarettes and was missing part of his right ring finger. A 9 mm sagged in his coat pocket, and he was one of the best pool players I'd ever seen. He also completed the daily crossword puzzle in a flash.

How well did King Lum teach me? Well, one day I hustled the king himself. He spotted me in Nine-Ball and I took him for sixty dollars. He never spoke to me or returned to Mike's again. People there whispered about what happened and the response was mixed.

Majority of the people there didn't like me, but most respected me. Hustling is a lonely business. Like King Lum said, "It's dog eat dog. You've got to screw them before they screw you." That sounded appropriate. That's how I perceived the world. King Lum simply honed my instincts and survival skills. When I took his money, it was like passing the final exam.

At Mike's, a businessman named Robert Chin stopped in from

time to time for a quick game of pool. Robert's about fifteen years older than me. I'd known him all my life, as our dads grew up together in China. Both families remained close even through our parents' strife.

Our fathers actually didn't speak to one another for more than twenty years over some trivial misunderstanding. I was amused by it. I know they didn't hate one another. In fact, my father and Uncle Bob, Sr., were political allies in Chinatown. They simply waited all those years for the other to speak first.

At least a dozen times, when they were together, I'd talk to both of them, trying to engage them in conversation. They were quite skilled in not conversing with one another. Both being powerful, influential men in the community, their egos got the best of them.

It wasn't until the last years of my father's life that they ended their silly dispute and made up. Robert, Jr., was also active in Chinatown affairs and made it known how my father supported him, referring to Daddy as his Chinatown *Dai Gall* or Big Brother.

One day I noticed a gang member who was a regular at Mike's gesturing to Robert as he whispered to his buddies standing nearby.

"That man over there is probably the last guy you'd want to fuck with," he said.

"Shit, he looks like he carries a lot of money," his companion responded. "Could be an easy target for me."

"You're a fuckin' idiot. Anyone who dares touch him is as good as dead. You don't have any idea who he is."

Robert, like myself, studied the *Choy Lay Fut* style of kung-fu and was quite good. I assumed that's what the other dude was referring to. But years later, Robert was indicted and named as a leader of one of the most powerful Tongs in America, with members linked to international organized crime.

I came to learn that Chinatown's powerful elite were the most unassuming, like my father's associates I thought were so boring. I was the closest to my father and only have a piece of the puzzle of who he was and what he was involved in. That's how he wanted it. I wonder how he felt knowing that his favorite son was following in his footsteps?

Trent and I had a friend named Brad who hung around Babe's. He was nicknamed "Bandito" because his coarse, curly hair and features made him look Hispanic. Although Bandito was American-born and didn't speak much Chinese, he was a Babe's guy who was regarded as one of their own by the foreign-borns.

I rarely shot pool at Babe's but stopped by there occasionally and shot dice with Babe himself.

"A Poor-Boy's sandwich and $10.00," I proposed.

He didn't talk much. If he was up to it, he'd take out the dice. If not, he'd ignore me.

Babe had an Italian kid, David, working alone one Saturday evening and the guy's older brother, John, about nineteen, stopped in. Bandito and John didn't take to each other. On the streets, it doesn't take much. Look at someone the wrong way and you've disrespected him. This can quickly lead to blows or a stand-off in which you really don't want to fight but you can't back down either.

So these two stood near the counter, shoulder to shoulder, ready to "go at it."

"Don't start anything, John," his brother pleaded.

"But I can take this guy."

"Yeah, and twenty guys are going to be on your ass, man!"

Bandito's buddies at Babe's weren't Wah Ching or Chung Yi members, but they were connected guys that you wouldn't want to mess with. Many were direct Tong members.

I surveyed the scene. Bandito was gripping a beer bottle by its neck behind his back and there were at least twenty-five guys ready to crack their cuesticks. John did the smart thing and backed down.

"Bandito, *da ma?*" (jump him?) one guy asked.

"Naw."

Out of respect for Babe and his establishment, Bandito let it go. Surely, if John had not relented, he would have received the beating of his life and possibly worse. I know I'd be in there getting my licks in. It's basically peer pressure and ego. On the streets, when fights broke out involving guys, you were ridiculed and ostracized for not joining in. Kudos are given to the ones applying the most damage. I couldn't survive on the streets if people thought I was afraid or my punches were no better than a "chick's."

After high school, Bandito became involved with a girl and they got into heated arguments. One day they got into a fight at his girlfriend's place, which led her neighbor to call the police. The cops arrived and took Bandito away. As soon as he was released, Bandito returned and confronted the neighbor. Within seconds, Bandito was dead from a .357 Magnum. The neighbor said Bandito was holding something behind his back and threatening to kill him. A knife was found beneath his body and the shooting was ruled "self-defense."

Some of the guys talked about going after the neighbor to avenge Bandito's death but I wasn't too surprised at the tragic end to his life. We were overly sensitive kids who responded to conflicts with violence. I accepted it as a fate many of us would fall victim to. Life wasn't fair, but honor had to be upheld—that's how it was in Chinatown.

I didn't attend my prom. My friends and I were late bloomers. Our hormones were raging but we had difficulty relating to girls. We preoccupied ourselves gambling and acting rowdy.

In my senior year, I was summoned to the Dean's office minutes before the morning session ended. Mr. Duvette, who had attempted to expel me during my sophomore year kept a close eye on me, in spite of my academic turnaround. A herculean man who stood at least 6'3," his muscles bulged through the same gray suit he wore Monday thru Friday. He patrolled the halls like a beat cop or prison guard. I had no idea what he wanted with me.

"Mr. Lee, we have information that you left the school grounds this morning, trespassed into another school and attacked a student there. The police are on their way."

"But that can't be," I replied. "I was in my classes this morning."

"Now listen here, young man," he snapped. "I already spoke to your first period teacher and he doesn't recall seeing you in class this morning. You and your friends must have driven over there after homeroom, beat-up the kid, and drove back here in time for second period."

"That's not true," I shouted.

"Well, can you prove where you were this morning?"

"I told you...I was in class! The teacher saw me and there were plenty of other kids around."

"Perhaps friends willing to lie for you?" Mr. Duvette added sarcastically.

Becoming angry, I knew I had to keep a straight head to clear this up. I couldn't believe my teacher didn't notice me that morning. As I stood nervously crumpling a bag of sunflower seeds in my jacket pocket, it occurred to me that there was a way to prove I was in class.

"Mr. Duvette, if we go to my first period class, I think I can prove I was there this morning."

"Well, you'd better not be wasting my time, son," he replied.

As we walked up to the second floor toward Mr. Cahill's class, the bell rang, ending the period. Kids passing us knew I was in hot water with the Dean serving as my escort. By the time we reached the room, the students had exited, leaving Mr. Cahill alone near the blackboard, where he was vigorously erasing away his notes.

"Bob, Mr. Lee here claims he was in class this morning," Mr. Duvette said.

"I'm sorry, but as I mentioned earlier, I can't recall seeing him," Mr. Cahill replied. "Unfortunately, I didn't have my attendance book with me this morning."

"Is that it, Mr. Lee?" Mr. Duvette asked. "You'd better give up your friends."

"Wait...look!" I yelled, pointing down toward the back of the class. On the floor, underneath the last desk on the center row, lay a pile of sunflower shells.

"What?! What?!" Mr. Duvette demanded to know.

My habit of chewing on sunflower seeds and littering the floor with shells irritated Mr. Cahill and drew complaints from the custodian who cleaned up after me every night. At that moment, my distasteful ritual was a godsend.

"Oh boy," Mr. Cahill voiced with concern. "William was in class this morning. He left a mess again. In fact, now I recall being disturbed by the crackling noises he made."

"See, I told you but no one would believe me," I exclaimed.

"I'm sorry, William," Mr. Cahill added.

"Well, I'm going to talk to the custodian to verify that he cleaned the room last night," Mr. Duvette remarked. "I still need to get to the bottom of this. I'm not through with you yet, Mr. Lee."

Man, what a jerk, I thought. *Why can't he just apologize? I should file a complaint against his sorry ass.*

That morning, some guys did ask me to help them jump some kids at another school, but I declined. I was making strong efforts to stay out of trouble and had developed other interests.

Mr. Duvette's innuendoes left me feeling like I should have gone and kicked some ass. But I couldn't let him get the best of me by acting like a punk. That would have given him an excuse to expel me.

At Galileo High, I got lazy changing to gym clothes for PE, so Trent suggested taking a tennis class.

"You get to wear regular clothes," he said, "as long as you have tennis shoes."

The sport became an essential part of my life. It provided a unique opportunity for me to socialize with diverse people in a competitive yet pleasant atmosphere. In time, I curtailed my late night carousing with the guys in order to get plenty of rest for early morning matches.

Due to a class assignment, I was required to view "King of Hearts" starring Alan Bates. I was touched by this classic film which presented a clever paradox of war and insanity. Before the movie began, a number of foreign films were previewed which piqued my interests. Soon I was hooked. The works of Lina Wertmuller, Claude Berri and François Truffaut moved me strongly. Not even Trent knew that I was sneaking away from Chinatown and sitting alone in a theater laughing and crying about the joys and pains of life and love. It was a nice change from the blood and gore films I was accustomed to.

Tennis and my private outings to the movies offered an escape from the pressures of family and the streets. I kept those activities a secret for fear they would be ruined or taken away from me. In hindsight, they probably saved me from jail or the undertaker.

CHAPTER 6.

"RIDING THE WATER," SECRET SOCIETY EXECUTIONS

On October 1, 1971, Joe Fong and his top guys resigned from Yow Lay and took about half the gang with them. It was a pivotal chapter in Chinatown's gang war. The very next day, one of Joe's best friends, Raymond Leung—regarded as one of the fiercest in the bunch—was killed in front of dozens of witnesses. He was chased through Chinatown, in and out of a store, and took a bullet. Still running, he finally collapsed on Grant Avenue and Jackson Street. One of his assailants walked up and delivered a *coup de grace* with two shots in the back of the head.

My father was having coffee near the scene. As a huge crowd gathered, he and his friends climbed onto the hood of a car to get a better view. He stumbled when he saw the body.

"Ah Chell!" He screamed out my name.

After my father's friends assured him that I was not the victim, he called home to make sure I was okay. I appreciated his concern but I was more interested in the murder. So I ran down to the crime scene. It was believed that outside hit men were brought in from the East Coast to hunt Joe and his lieutenants down.

A new war was declared, and I was concerned for many of my friends who remained loyal to Joe. They were now taking on the Hock Sair Woey, the Chinese Underworld. Shortly after Raymond's murder, three others from their group were abducted and executed. Their bodies were disposed of in the manner of secret societies' rituals. All had been beaten, strangled and "hog tied." Two were found in the bay, known as "riding the water." It was the beginning of a war that over the next six years claimed close to fifty lives.

In Chinese literature, there is a popular story set in the seventeenth century titled "The Water Margin." The tale centers on a band of outlaws in the mountains near Shantung. They took money from oppressive government officials and lived by the credo, *Chung Yi,* Loyalty & Righteousness.

On Chinese New Year, 1972, Joe Fong and his friends formed a new group and adopted the name Chung Yi. In time, they were simply known as "Joe Boys."

My sister May began working for the Chinatown Youth Service Center in early '71. Counseling and intervention were her primary duties. Clients ranged from truants to suspected murderers, and her work crossed over the warring gangs. May was very savvy. She grew up around fei jies (gangsters) and had deep empathy for them. She was well-liked and respected.

Around the middle of the year, her boss resigned and a new director was hired from outside Chinatown. I recall meeting Brendan Low at their office on Columbus Avenue, where I frequently visited May.

"Brendan, this is my brother, William."

"Nice to meet you," Brendan said.

"Yeah, same here."

As he darted away, I recall being impressed. He was a straight-up guy, not pretentious at all. Brendan was also friendly and charming.

At the same time, there was an intensity to him. He was completely engrossed in the place.

Brendan called our home often to speak with my sister. She was impressed with his passion and energy.

"Brendan's a good guy," May commented. "He's smart and really cares. I just hope he doesn't get used."

The man had wonderful ideas and was genuinely concerned about the kids. He wanted to know everything about Chinatown, including the illicit activities. My observation and concern was that he was trying to be everyone's buddy. In time, Brendan became privy to sensitive information about the gangs. The problem was that trust was very delicate, especially since he served as confidante to warring groups. These guys survived by being very cautious. Brendan's intent wasn't to take on the Hock Sair Woey. He just wanted to end the gang war.

Tension mounted as he was scheduled to be interviewed on a popular radio program June 26, approximately one year after he took the job. The topic was Chinatown, and Brendan devised a plan to end the violence. He confronted both gangs, threatening to reveal information if they didn't end their dispute. He let it be known that he was serious and awaited their answer. My sister was one of the few people aware of what Brendan was up to. She was uncomfortable with his plan from the start.

"William, what do you think of what Brendan's doing?" May asked.

"Listen," I replied. "There's no way they're going to be forced into ending anything. He's basically telling them that he's betraying them. You know how these people think. They don't care that he means well. Tell him to drop it. And you better watch yourself, May! You don't want them to think this was your idea or that you were in on it."

The evening of the interview, Brendan telephoned my sister. "They didn't respond," a dejected Brendan said. "I've decided not to go on the air."

Unfortunately, no one knew this. Perhaps it wouldn't have mattered. He was suddenly perceived as a loose cannon. The fact that Brendan previously worked in the probation department fueled their suspicion of him.

"He's not going on the show," May announced.

I was anxious to hear what he had to say on the program, but knew he made the right decision. So I went to bed.

The following morning, I woke up and noticed May in my room, sleeping on the spare bed. My mother walked in and I asked, *"Jo mut yea ah?"* (What's going on?)

"Someone murdered May's boss!" my mother whispered frantically. *"She got a call in the middle of the night. She was afraid to be alone so she fell asleep in your room."*

Shit, I thought. *And he didn't even go on the program.*

I wanted to stay home with my sister, but my mother insisted that I go to school. It was all over the news. Kids were talking about it at Galileo.

Brendan, twenty-nine, was killed in his home just after eleven p.m. as he answered his door. Shot three times in the head and once in the chest and abdomen, he was DOA at Park Emergency Hospital.

A note found under his body read, "Pig Informers Die Yong" (sic). Someone took Brendan's threat seriously.

May was waiting anxiously to speak with me when I got home.

"Did you hear who may have killed Brendan?" she asked.

"A lot of people were talking about it. Some were saying Joe Boys, while others were sure it was Wah Chings. They're just guessing. Hell...maybe both gangs were in on it together," I said facetiously.

"Try to find out, okay?"

"Are you nuts, May?! Snoop around and get myself killed! Hell no!"

I knew she was concerned but I couldn't believe she wanted me to stick my neck out. It's one thing to hear information on the streets, but asking questions can be suicide.

Some believe he was killed simply because he knew too much. Others felt he had no business being in Chinatown. There was suspicion that he was sent in to infiltrate the gangs. To me, Brendan was a community worker with the greatest intentions who got in way over his head. He risked and lost his life trying to stop a war involving players more ruthless than he imagined.

My sisters, Mary and May, both dated their share of fei jies (gangsters). In early '72, May was dating Patrick Kwok, a Wah Ching and Yow Lay member who was an enemy of Chung Yi. He was known on the streets as *"Gwai Geen Sow,"* which translates to "Ghosts Fear Him." Things got interesting when May broke up with Patrick and started dating Eddie Young, a Chung Yi member who was very close to Joe Fong. These guys were at war and now they were threatening each other, using me as their messenger.

"Gwai Geen Sow, my ass!" Eddie screamed. "Nobody fears him. We used to call him *Heung Ha Lo* [China Man] and had to teach him how to dress. You tell him I want to see him."

"Shit, Eddie got the name *'Dai How'* [Big Mouth] because you can never shut him up. You tell him, anytime!" Patrick replied.

When I first met Eddie, he was facing attempted kidnapping charges for a Wah Ching associate who had testified in a case against Joe. Although Eddie had been in a lot of trouble, I got to know him quite well and enjoyed his company. We used to sit in front of my house and talk for hours. Both Patrick and Eddie were aware of my father, and Eddie didn't hesitate to tease me about it.

"I'm going to Mike's. You wanna come?" he'd ask. "You wanna go eat with the guys later? Ha...Ha. Everyone in Chinatown knows you're 'hands off.' If your father saw us trippin' together, he'd kill you!"

My father was notably more lenient with the girls. But when it came to his precious sons, he was much more protective.

Eddie cared a great deal about my sister, as well as his friends. He had dropped out of high school and had a very bleak outlook on his future.

"I can't get a good job here," Eddie said. "Look at my mom. Works her ass off for what? You think I'm going to do the same thing?"

"You're a smart guy, Eddie," I said. "Why not go to night school? You have skills and you can do something with your life. You gotta believe in yourself, man."

Of course, his friends meant more to him than anything. They were his adopted family and there was a war going on. His blood-brothers were getting killed and he wasn't going to stand idly by. Eddie and my sister broke up after six months. From that point on, my contact with him was infrequent.

I ran into him a few months later at North Beach Playground, where I played tennis. He was leading a group of about thirty-five Joe Boys and they were goofin' off.

"What's happenin', Eddie?"

"Nothin' much, we're just runnin' around, looking for Wah Chings and fuckin' with people." I didn't doubt him. They were a rough looking bunch with trouble written all over 'em.

One of the kids with Eddie was Lincoln Louie, who at fifteen was highly respected in the gang. We recognized each other and exchanged courtesy nods. Unfortunately, Lincoln was one of the worst tragedies of the war. Standing at a bus stop with his girlfriend on Stockton Street in Chinatown, April 1974, Lincoln was kidnapped by Wah Chings. They took him out of town and brutally tortured him before he was killed. What they did to him was inhumane and violated all the rules of conventional war. It made me shiver when I heard what he endured.

This war brought out the savagery in people. One of his killers was Michael "Hot Dog" Louie, who was convicted as a juvenile for the murder.

On the night of August 12, 1973, Wayne Fung, a top member of the Wah Ching, was gunned down at a gas station near Golden Gate

Park, where he worked as an attendant. He was a scary guy who "hot-rodded" around in a car riddled with bullet holes. Just the roar of his car coming down the street frightened people. Wayne made a name for himself and had plenty of enemies. Many of my friends were being extorted by him for money and fireworks.

The following year, a grand jury indicted four Joe Boys in connection with the killing of Wayne. Four other members were given immunity and provided complete details of the crime.

In what was described as a "carefully planned and rehearsed murder," Eddie was named as the actual trigger man. During preparations, diagrams had been drawn; getaway cars were carefully positioned, and stop signs were noted in the escape route. A choice of weapons was presented along with specific execution instructions. Disposal of the .380 Llama automatic pistol was also planned. Eddie was subsequently convicted of first-degree murder and conspiracy to commit murder.

On April 15, 1975, during Eddie's sentencing, the judge stated that if the killing had occurred after reinstatement of the death penalty (in 1974), "I probably would be sentencing you to the gas chamber." Instead, he pronounced a life sentence.

Eddie's involvement didn't surprise me yet I felt bad for him and wished the Judge and jury knew him the way I did. Nevertheless, Eddie had to pay for his deed. The fact that Chung Yi members testified against their own was a real disgrace to the group that was founded on the principle of loyalty.

According to grand jury testimony, the killing of Wayne Fung was planned around the dinner table in the home of Gene Fong,

Joe's eldest brother. By the time the district attorney issued the indictments, Gene had already been murdered.

It was Monday afternoon, April 29, 1974, and I was driving through Chinatown after attending classes at San Francisco State. As I approached an intersection, I heard a woman screaming. Looking over, a body was sprawled on the ground in front of a meat market on the corner of Stockton and Pacific. Without a second thought, I pulled over and immediately recognized the woman standing over the lifeless body.

It was Gene Fong's wife. She was crying hysterically. Massive blood spewing from the victim flowed over the sidewalk and onto the street. From my car, I stepped up to the edge of the blood and confirmed that it was Gene.

People huddled around whispering, while others were notably shaken by what they saw. One woman walking by with a small child shielded his eyes. A butcher from the market was an eyewitness.

"Ngor jheir ga kai di sern haer don hi jook um doe!" (I chased the bastard up the street but couldn't catch him!) he shouted. A friend of Gene's, the butcher had gone after the gunman, armed with a meat cleaver.

Would he have chopped up the gunman? I wondered. *The killer could have killed the butcher as well. What's going to happen to Gene's children? And Joe...he's in prison. How's he going to react?*

After Gene's body was removed, a worker from the market came out and washed the sidewalk. I stood and watched as water gushing from his hose saturated the blood. Suddenly my mind flashed back to another execution-style hit I stumbled upon.

A year earlier, my family and I met for Sunday dinner in Chinatown. We were celebrating my graduation from high school. May and I drove together, and as usual, we were running late.

We found a parking space on Grant Avenue across from the restaurant. As I opened the passenger door to exit on the street side, a police officer on a motorcycle zoomed by. He came within an inch of the door.

"What the fuck...?" I yelled. May and I soon realized that something was going on up the street. "Ooh, let's go look," I said.

As we reached the corner, I noticed a man's shoe on the pavement near the gutter. Twenty feet away, a dead body was sprawled in the intersection. Blood was seeping from the man's head. I noticed that the victim's sports jacket and pants were outdated and mismatched. His hair was unkempt. He appeared to be in his late thirties.

"Hey May, this guy doesn't look like anybody connected" I said. "Know him?"

"No," she responded. "Let's go. I don't want to stay here."

More police officers and an ambulance arrived as we entered Louie's Restaurant. I was worked up and reported what I saw to the other family members while May was noticeably quiet and reserved.

I figured, *What's the big deal? We've seen plenty of other victims. I'm sure not going to lose sleep over this. I can't believe May's acting like a wimp.*

I came to understand that my sister's reaction was natural and much healthier than my response. I simply disassociated from it like everything else traumatic in my childhood.

In time, those violent images would reappear and haunt me.

Indeed, it would be virtually impossible to sleep without demons replaying endless violent scenes that were embedded in my memory.

The victim was Yip Yee Tak, a.k.a. Dr. Ysung Yang, a reputed Wah Ching leader. Witnesses stated that the assailant chased him for two blocks, shooting him in the back as they approached the corner. As the victim lay on the ground, the killer grabbed him by the collar and pumped two more shots into his head. The gun, with no hand grips, was recovered in a nearby alley.

Chol Soo Lee, a native of Korea, was arrested and convicted of the murder. While serving his sentence, he was accused of killing another inmate. He won a retrial, and the Chinatown murder conviction was overturned. His story was the basis for the 1989 film "True Believer," which starred James Woods and Robert Downey, Jr.

CHAPTER 7.

JOE BOYS

Approaching the end of 1975, I was in my third year at S.F. State, majoring in Psychology, consistently making the Dean's List. Joe Fong, Cal, Eddie and at least half a dozen others in the gang were still serving out their time at Dalton State Prison.

May was working at Chinese Youth Alternatives, another program emphasizing diversion and intervention for "at-risk" Chinese youths. The organization was headed by Wylie Yip, a close friend of Joe Fong. CYA provided martial arts classes and job placement assistance. They also attracted kids by organizing dances, sports and recreational activities. Casework involved kids who got in trouble with the law. Many were referred by juvenile court judges and probation officers.

My father and I took a trip to the Orient during the summer, just the two of us. My intention was to watch over him, but our relationship deteriorated. I finally took a stand, no longer willing to put up with his drunken, abusive behavior. The manipulation—using guilt to control me—was resented.

At the age of twenty one, I was tired of being the honorable son, chosen martyr in the family, which meant my wishes and needs didn't matter. Although I was doing well in school and with my part-time job, I was still drawn to the streets. I was ready to step across the line into the gangs. And with so many friends who were Joe Boys, I had already been "labeled."

One evening, May and I were at a downtown pool hall when a fight broke out. Some Joe Boys were in the middle section shooting pool. Another group of Asian kids was at a front table near the jukebox. We were in the back section. As one of the Joe Boys was coming out of the bathroom, he passed a guy from the other group. They stopped and had a stare-down, directly in front of us. The music was blaring.

"What the fuck you looking at?!" the Joe Boy shouted.

"I ain't looking at shit!" was the response. "What the fuck you looking at?!" They had never crossed paths before. But just like that— they went at it. Both were on the ground, punching and wrestling. Immediately other Joe Boys jumped in. As the guy was held down, Joe Boys cracked cuesticks across his head. The other fella's friends just stood there.

My sister, the youth advocate, intervened. She threw herself on the guy to buffer him from the blows. I jumped in to protect her. When the fighting ended, the guy's head was split open. May and I had his blood splattered all over us.

After the Joe Boys ran off, the fella's buddies were suddenly ready to act tough and fight. *Where were they when he needed them?*

May and I went outside when we heard the proprietor calling the police. Right then, I glanced up the street and saw the Joe Boys, five of them, running back toward us. Each had a hand on his waist and they were using their jackets to conceal something. I knew they were packing and coming back for more. The leader was in front. I stopped him and held his arms down.

"Be cool, man," I whispered. "The cops are coming."

"Fuck 'em. I just need a few seconds to take care of that ass hole. No punk's gonna fuck with me."

"Hey, don't do it. You've already kicked his ass good. Come on just go...for me, man," I pleaded.

He paused and looked me straight in the eye. "Alright," he said. *"Jow la"* [let's go], he ordered. They retreated to a waiting car at the corner.

It wasn't the first time I diffused a crisis. The other fella, now with a towel draped around his head, had no idea how close he and his friends came to being sent to their graves.

The next week, word got back to me that the guys I saved were going to come after me for knowing the Joe Boys. *How ironic,* I thought. But that's the risk you take in getting involved. The streets are full of misunderstandings. I wasn't worried. You learn to distinguish guys on the streets who are all talk. Those wannabes were just trying to save face for "punking out" on their friend. If they made a move against me, my friends would have been more than happy to finish where they left off.

At least a dozen mini-groups made up the Joe Boys gang, with each comprised of ten to twenty solid members. Each had its own hierarchy and operated somewhat independently, with many communicating through older members or group leaders. I began to spend time with many of them, yet I was most attracted to a group led by Tim Yuen, who was just sixteen. An intelligent kid, with soft, innocent looks, he was a strategist with a violent penchant. He and his boys were volatile and the most feared. There was a real sense of power being with those guys. Most of them looked up to me because I was in college and grew up with many of the older members.

Ironically, my first run-in with Tim and his guys was during a fight. It started at a crowded dance I attended with May, her future husband, Don, their friend Sean and his girlfriend, Jeanne. It was held at Kabuki Hall next to the Miyako Hotel in Japantown. Most of the party-goers were from Chinatown. Sean had close friends who were Hop Sing Boys, allied with the Wah Chings. Trent, my old partner, was there with his friends and so were other groups of Joe Boys. I knew all of them with the exception of the younger ones.

As the dance ended at one a.m., we stepped out of the hall and began walking on Post Street to our car. I nodded to Trent as we passed him and noticed some younger Joe Boys including Tim Yuen, ahead of us leaning on parked cars. There were about nine of them and none looked to be older than sixteen. I was walking alongside Don and my sister with Sean and Jeanne just behind us.

As we passed them, someone yelled, "Mother fucker!" Next, Jeanne screamed, "Stop it!" I turned and saw Sean being attacked. Don yelled, "Hey!" and pulled a kid off Sean. "Cool it man!" I shouted as I grabbed another one and shoved him aside.
"Trent...get over here!" I yelled.

May got hold of one guy and they fell to the ground. Jeanne climbed on the back of another one and was wailing away with her fists. Trent jumped in, immediately grabbed Tim, and everyone stopped.

"What the fuck's wrong with you?!" Trent shouted. Tim wouldn't look at Trent. He just stared at Sean and yelled, "Fuck you, man!"

"Fuck you, too!" Sean snapped. "You need this many people to jump me?! Let's see how tough you are! Just you and me!"

"You guys want to fight, do it fair. One-on-one," Don added.

Tim lunged at Sean but Trent held him.

"That's enough! Get outta here!" Trent shouted as he pushed Tim away.

Tim and his boys finally backed off and began walking in the opposite direction. As we went on our way, I held my breath as a Dodge Charger slowly cruised by us with its windows rolled down.

As we reached our car, Sean swore he would go after them. May suffered the worst casualty. When she fell, her jade bracelet hit the pavement and shattered into pieces.

The next day I stopped by Trent's to talk about what happened and found myself curious about those young rowdies.

"What's with them, Trent?"

"Well, they do a lot for the group. They're just pretty wild and get out of control."

The next week Tim, as directed by his elders, apologized to May and offered payment to replace the bracelet. Sean went to the Hop Sing Boys and they helped him retaliate. They attacked a couple of Tim's guys who weren't even at the dance. With an all-out order to go after Sean, Trent stepped in and diffused the situation. But in doing so, he lost considerable respect within the gang.

I was formally introduced to Tim and Matt Yuen at the Town and Country Pool Hall on Mission Street by Robert Lew, a member of Eddie Young's group. "This is William. You guys remember fighting with him?"

Matt, who has the same surname as Tim but is not related, responded, "Shiiit man... you lucky I wasn't there. I would have kicked everyone's ass. So are you Tow Gee [American-born]?" he asked, looking directly at me.

"Ngor hai Tow Gee don hai ngor tone nay gong Gong Dhown Wah" (I was born here but I'll speak Cantonese with you), I replied.

"That's pretty good," Matt said. "You sure you born here?"

"Hey, we hear you're good in kung fu...how tough are you?" Tim asked.

"Well, let's just say I started very young."

"You learned with Cal, right? He's one bad mother fucker, man. No one dares mess with him," Tim said. "Man, you guys used to get in a lot of fights, huh?"

"Your sister May is pretty cool too," Matt said.

Matt wore his hair in an Afro, and all of them were wearing polyester shirts, bell-bottom pants, and platform shoes with four-inch heels. They looked cold and hard, as though they didn't care about anything or anyone.

"William, we're gonna go play miniature golf," Robert said. "You wanna come or stay here?"

"I'm cool here, man...thanks. I'll talk to you tomorrow. I'll call you."

I knew Tim and "the guys" were checking me out and I wanted to give them the opportunity. It didn't take long for them to accept me. After that evening, the issue of being an ABC never came up again.

Once I hooked up with these guys, I led a double life. Friends and colleagues knew me as a college student, conscientious employee and enthusiastic tennis player, while others feared and despised me as a hardcore gangster. Once I became a Joe Boy, I knew my father wouldn't be able to protect me any longer. No one gets a free ride in the Hock Sair Woey.

The first night I went out with Tim's group was an eye-opening experience. Someone suggested going to the beach. We had three carloads full of guys, and when we arrived, there was a large gathering of kids there. After standing around for a few minutes, I noticed the guys removing baseball bats and crowbars out of a trunk.

"What's going on?" I asked.

"Oh, we see someone from school that we don't like," Peter replied casually.

My God, I thought. *They're going to kill the guy.*

As they started moving toward this kid, a police car pulled up with the spotlight shining. The guys quickly put their weapons away and we drove off. I don't think their intended victim realized the close call he had. The cops just wanted to clear the area, and I was actually glad they showed up.

In addition to Tim, the main players in the group were his brothers Dale (nick-named "Mad Dog") and Chad; Matt and his partner Peter; Carl and his brother Don. Paul Ng, Mitch, Gan Wah Woo, a.k.a. Ah Wah, and a feisty kid we called "Tiger" were also core members. The guys frequently called one another "cuz," short for cousin, which affirmed our bond.

Back then, most of us had body perms on our hair and wore *Mien Nop* (Mao-type) silk jackets. The large pockets came in handy for carrying weapons. While most of the guys looked hostile and dangerous, some of us purposely projected unassuming appearances. When something "went down," we'd pretend to be simple bystanders, offering ourselves as eye witnesses in order to provide conflicting information.

Our group numbered close to forty, while another Joe Boy faction with a similar profile was headed by Gerrick Wong, seventeen. The majority were foreign-born, but the gang was founded on the principle of ABCs and FOBs united in the brotherhood.

In spike of the fact that these were rowdy teenagers, everyone got along fairly well. Camaraderie was emphasized, and conflicts that arose were usually settled by having the kids spar during kung-fu practice. Bad feelings were also settled by playing basketball.

There were regular games at the Chinese Center between Tim's and Gerrick's boys. Guys who had personal grudges went after one another on the court. We usually let them "duke" it out. Others who were seeking protection in the group, and not daring or willing to fight, were screened out.

A tattoo artist named Bruce Romero befriended many of the Joe Boys. Some of them bore his designs on their arms and chests. He even began teaching Tim the trade. After a dare, I agreed to have a dragon tattooed on my arm. Luckily, we never got around to it.

A kid named Tracy also popped up from time to time. He worked after school in a drugstore and was stealing Valiums and Quaaludes. Some of the guys were into drugs. Tracy would come by and turn everyone on, just give his stash away. When he got fired, he was only concerned with getting the facts straight.

"My boss said 1,200 Quaaludes were missing," Tracy shouted. "Fuck, I probably stole 900 at most. He can't blame me for the other 300! I'm going to straighten this out."

We all sat there laughing our heads off. He was so loaded he hadn't realized he no longer had a job.

Kids beginning in middle school and younger were targeted for recruitment. If you weren't afraid of being locked up or getting hurt, and could keep your mouth shut with the authorities, you passed muster. The rebellious period these juveniles were going through at home and at school played to the gang's advantage. Many felt self-conscious and usually gained confidence by joining up. Some were bullied and had scores to settle. The majority were angry and frustrated, lacking skills to deal with their emotions constructively, including myself.

Virtually all of us resented our parents. Families who emigrated here got a rude awakening, expecting the Gum Shan (Gold Mountain) to offer a better, more prosperous life; instead they faced limited opportunities and discrimination, often by their own countrymen. Instead of admiring our dads and moms who worked long hours to stay afloat, we turned their absence into a sense of neglect or outright abandonment, which manifested as anger. Kids realized that running away from home wasn't necessary, since no one was usually in the house. When we stayed out late, no one seemed to care.

Society regards hard-working Chinese as the "model minority," but our family system was compromised. The guys who turned to the gangs were desperately seeking identity and empowerment. Most were willing to do anything to be accepted. Without a doubt, our self-esteem were lacking to begin with. We also desired the finer things that represented status and success, but we were ashamed of our parents working "coolie" jobs. It's as though they failed us. We wanted cars, clothes and cash to come fast and easy. And we wanted to live on our terms and make up our own rules. There was no reason to be good little boys and play fair—the dark side seemed more attractive.

Guys didn't get "jumped in" to be a member or "jumped out" to leave the gang. Secret societies (from which Triads and Tongs were derived) whose origins date back to the first century, A.D. in China, had specific initiation rituals and by-laws which demanded allegiance for life. Members who switched to a different clan or committed other acts of betrayal faced death. But with the independent gangs I became involved with, they were traditional, yet less formal. Animals were not sacrificed and ceremonies were not always a prerequisite. That didn't mean a guy could just walk in and out. Members who were critically wounded or served hard time on behalf of the gang earned exit passes.

Reformed kids learned that being labeled and connected had serious liabilities. Once you've made enemies, you relied on the gang for protection. Putting the word out that "so-and-so" was no longer affiliated meant it was open season on him. Most who gave up the gang were forced to move away. Keep in mind that these gangs were organized and had chapters in virtually all major Chinese communities. If you became privy to sensitive information on the group, you were vulnerable. These guys survived by being extremely careful, and trust didn't come easily. They couldn't afford to have underlings out there suddenly developing a conscience who may turn against them. Keeping close track of the members was mandatory. Instilling fear was a common deterrent.

The Chinese Underworld had its own idiosyncrasies. I was surprised by how superstitious most of the guys were. Sure, they would abide by established codes. But other factors also regulated their behavior. For instance, it was bad luck to commit a crime when it was raining. Debts were settled prior to year's end. Conflicts were avoided the first week of the new year. The mourning period following death of members was also sacred.

Statues of Guan Dai, the God of War, were positioned high on the premises of businesses to guard against shoplifters, robbers and other negative forces. The belief was that those who misbehaved faced the spiritual wrath of this hero. Some of us took this seriously, especially since Guan Dai was also our protector in the underworld.

I actually returned stolen knives from a store after being up all night with Guan Dai's image haunting me. His intimidating figure was more of a deterrent than guards, alarms or video cameras. It felt silly returning to the shop the following day, discreetly taking the goods out of my pocket and placing them back on the shelf. Yet, I convinced myself that it was the only way to make amends to Guan Dai.

Functioning in the gang meant maintaining a low profile to avoid attention with the police, while projecting an intimidating image on the streets. We usually moved in large numbers but took different routes to reach our destination. Before entering a restaurant, nightclub, theater or pool hall, reconnaissance was necessary. The first group to arrive checked the place out and scouted for familiar cars in a two to three-block radius. We purposely sat apart from one another with no more than four people together. In a theater, for example, if one group was attacked or got in a fight, their opponents would be ambushed from all sides.

New recruits were taught to jump their prey from behind, pulling the victim's jacket over his head as the attack was launched. This not only pinned the person's arms and disoriented him, it prevented identification of the perpetrators.

If cops showed up and questioned or arrested one group, they would be on their own. We didn't know them and they'd never seen us before. When it came time to leave, the drivers accompanied by another person retrieved the cars and picked up the rest of the passengers. We didn't exit the establishments until our rides arrived. These precautions were not done for dramatics. It was all part of the survival game.

Citizen-band radios were popular in the mid-1970s. Some of our younger members enjoyed jabbering on them, and it nearly got them killed. Once, during an exchange of dialogue between two groups of Joe Boys in separate cars, they gave away their destination. That prompted a group of Wah Chings listening in to set up an ambush.

The younger members and girls who tagged along carried the guns. Girls were welcomed and exploited for sex but having a girlfriend was discouraged. Your blood-brothers always came first. Other relationships were discouraged. The gang didn't want to compete with outside influences, especially someone telling them to stay out of trouble. Girls were referenced in sexist, derogatory terms:

"So and so's got themselves a bitch."

"Are you going to let a bitch tell you what to do?"

"Are you scared of your bitch?"

"Bitches are a dime-a-dozen."

"Your bitch is turning you into a wimp, man."

The guys saw me with dates on various occasions and gave me an ear-full.

Girls involved with us were also quite violent. They didn't hesitate to use knives, sharpened combs or fingernails to disfigure their enemies. I saw fights between girls where dresses were ripped open and underwear virtually torn off. Dangling pierced earrings were also yanked off creating a bloody mess. Of course, guys provoked them into these "cat fights."

It was acceptable for older members to have girlfriends and wives. Having a "drop-dead" gorgeous "old lady" was a status symbol. But the gang should always remain your first priority.

In time, I became Tim's driver and we were usually accompanied by Peter, Matt and Paul. Although we got a kick out of being rowdy, there were times our frolicking went too far.

We were on the freeway late one night in a caravan with three other cars strategically distanced. Earth, Wind & Fire's *That's the Way of the World* was shrilling out of the eight speakers. Suddenly a driver was tailgating and flashing their high-beams at me.

"Some mother fucker's on my ass," I shouted.

From the rear-view mirror, I could see that it was a young, white couple. The man was driving. Matt and Peter were in the back seat of our car. Both turned around and began screaming.

"Hey fuck you man! You want to die?! Get the fuck outta here!"

"Turn off your lights, cuz..." Tim said.

"What...my lights?"

"Yea, you'll see."

I turned off my headlights.

"Okay, put them back on."

"Alright, now what?" I asked.

"Slow down," Tim said.

Within seconds, my comrades got the signal and approached with their cars. We suddenly had the vehicle behind me boxed in on four sides. The guys were blaring their horns, screaming profanities and pointing guns. We slowed down to about fifteen miles per hour. I turned off my lights so the driver behind couldn't read my license plate. The man was at our mercy.

"Aha, the guy's shitting in his pants," Peter shouted.

We finally gave him room to escape, with a humble lesson in defensive driving. That was our own version of "road rage."

One Friday afternoon, Carl and Don's father took us for a cruise in a friend's limousine. I sat up front with Carl and his father while Tiger, Don, Tim, Matt and Peter were in the back.

On Lombard Street, we stopped at a signal. A red truck with three white kids who looked to be in their late teens pulled up next to us on the left side. The two passengers looked over and pulled the corners of their eyes back. The one closest to us began making racist comments.

"I eat chop suey...I'm a Chinaman...you like fortune-cookie?"

"Hey fuck you!" we shouted in unison.

Carl and Don's father stopped us, and said, "Leave them bigots alone. They're not worth it." The red truck stayed side by side with us and the occupants continued their obnoxious behavior.

Tiger, who sat to the far right, passed something to Don, who handed it to Tim, who placed it with Matt and it finally reached Peter. He lowered the window and stuck a gun out. He pulled the trigger back. I looked over and saw one of them mouth, "Holy shit" as the truck peeled rubber and screeched away.

Mr. Lew didn't know what happened and commented, "Shit, those guys acted like they saw a ghost." We just sat back, grinned, and exchanged high-fives.

I thought, *Yea, that'll teach them ass holes. No one messes with us.*

Early one morning, around two a.m., we were heading home on Pacific Avenue. Suddenly a Mustang accelerated past me on the left side, and into the on-coming traffic. Cutting back into my lane, the vehicle swiped the front of my car. The driver sped away and I gave chase, blasting my horn. We both ran through a stop sign without slowing down. Then from the corner of my eye, I heard, then saw Dale's Dodge Charger race past me. He cut the Mustang off with ease.

About ten of us stormed out of the cars and confronted the driver. I restrained the guys from attacking him. Right away, we could tell he was intoxicated. As the guys surrounded him, I ran to the corner and called the police. As we waited, most of the guys, especially Matt, had second thoughts.

"We know who he is and where he lives," Matt said. "Why don't we let him go?"

"But I'm worried that he'll drive off and kill somebody," I said.

"Yea, but it's fucked up to be locked up," Matt added.

When the officer arrived, the guys were actually amused and enjoyed conversing with him. They were on the other side for once, not being detained or arrested.

Guns were the weapons of choice. From revolvers, automatic pistols, semi-automatic rifles to shotguns, by the mid-70s, gangs in Chinatown had easy access to firearms in all sizes, shapes and calibers. Virtually everyone had a source. Some of the middle school kids were rewarded with guns.

Stephen Lam, thirteen, a student at Marina Middle School, was being groomed to head up his own Joe Boy group. One day his mom was going through his room and found a loaded .22 revolver. She had never seen or touched a gun in her life.

Mrs. Lam picked it up and inadvertently pulled the trigger back, locking it into firing position. She was stunned and didn't know what to do. She gently placed the gun in her purse and ran around the neighborhood looking for Stephen or any of his friends to help her. She ruled out going to the police or telling her husband for fear of bringing attention to Stephen. Mrs. Lam finally arrived at Tiger's house and he took the gun from her. She insisted that he keep it. It's a miracle the .22 didn't go off as Mrs. Lam was transporting it.

We really put our parents through hell. Many felt guilty not being there for us, and they assumed that if they worked hard, the family would be fine. Attorney fees, jail visitations and funerals weren't exactly what they had in mind.

I had my fair share of guns pointed at me. Once a cop who was frisking me had his shotgun pushed up against the side of my head. I saw his index finger stiffening up. I knew if I bumped the barrel or if his finger twitched, my brains would have been splattered. But nothing shook me more than when one of my sisters pointed a snub-nose .38 at me point blank, assuming it was unloaded.

"Don't point that thing at me!" I screamed.

"What's the big deal, it's empty," she replied.

Her husband quickly grabbed the gun, opened the cylinder and displayed a fully loaded revolver. She almost killed her kid brother. I never pointed a gun at anything unless I was about to shoot it.

Drive-bys occurred but the traffic congestion in Chinatown limited it as a regular mode of attack. Quite a number of killings involved assailants on foot who maneuvered into close range, hit their target, then disappeared into the crowd.

Cars were also torched in the war. Once, Dave Tam of the Hop Sing Boys parked his beautiful, white mid-60s Chevrolet Impala in front of Matt's house in North Beach. This occurred shortly after one of our cars had been firebombed. Most of the warring gang members knew where one another resided. Yet, when he returned, Dave was shocked to find his pride and joy toasted to the ground.

In the mid-1970s, the San Francisco Police went out on strike, and the Chinese Underworld capitalized on the opportunity. Virtually all gangs were involved in the crime spree. Jewelry stores in Chinatown were hit, restaurants and garment factories were robbed, and selective looting took place. It was anarchy, but most of the crimes went unreported. It didn't do any good—police were not adequately staffed and police reports weren't needed since most businesses were uninsured. In fact, many of the establishments had their own secrets to conceal and didn't want to risk drawing attention to themselves.

Liang jies (punks) were known to enter bars and restaurants, extorting the owners by simply sitting one per table. By doing so, they virtually shut down the establishment. Without lifting a finger, their message was delivered—no payoff, no customers!

When we ventured out, money wasn't needed, especially if we stayed around Chinatown. At nightclubs, people were always buying us drinks to get on our good side. Some owned businesses and wished to be left alone, while others wanted to appear connected with us.

When we ate out, one of us would simply sign his name on the bill. Once, about twenty of us had sil yeh (late snack) at Sai Yon's on Jackson Street. When the check came, Peter went through each item with the restaurant manager, questioning the prices and demanding that certain dishes be deducted because they didn't meet our standards. He even suggested how each dish could have been better prepared. After a lengthy dialogue, the manager agreed to adjust the charges.

"Okay, gum jow ngam la" (Okay, now it's correct), Peter said, and simply scribbled his name on the check.

We couldn't stop laughing as the manager wore the most disgusted look on his face. He knew when we walked in that we had no intention of paying for our meal. Haggling over the bill and insulting the chef was just rubbing it in his face and dishonoring him.

I knew if the restaurant was Tong-affiliated, our actions could be perceived as an insult, provoking them to come after us. At the very least, there were consequences. I didn't eat much during those stunts and avoided my father when I got home.

When we attended local dances, promoters and the "rent-a-cops" were usually intimidated. We often walked in without paying and strutted onto the middle of the dance floor, staring people down. The music usually stopped and patrons quickly cleared the area. That made me feel important . We fooled ourselves into believing we were better than anyone else and did whatever we pleased.

The Great Highway near Ocean Beach was a popular gathering spot and showcase for macho boys and their "souped-up" cars. Late Friday and Saturday nights, guys converted the two lanes into a drag strip. GTOs, 'Cudas, Camaro Z28's, Nomads, 'Vettes and Cobras were all tuned, waxed and loaded with eight-tracks or cassettes. Drivers had to guard against water, soda or orange juice being poured into their gas tanks by saboteurs. (Once, I saw a guy remove the gas cap of an opponent's vehicle and urinate into it.) Racing for pinks slips was common. I always wondered how those hot-rodders explained to their parents the sudden loss of their vehicles.

The guys got in a lot of fights, many of which I took issue with. One afternoon, I arrived at the Chinese Center, and a Joe Boy group under the command of Gerrick Wong was standing outside.

"What's going on?" I asked.

David, one of Gerrick's leaders replied, "You know Jason Fung, right?"

"Yea, why...did something happen?"

"He just pulled a gun on Gerrick and almost shot him."

"Here?! What was Jason doing here?!"

"Earlier, some punk was walking by acting like he was bad so we jumped him. He came back with his brother."

"Then what?" I asked.

"The dude walked right up to Gerrick, put a gun to his head and said, 'If you ever touch my baby brother again, I'll kill you...I don't care who the fuck you are?!'"

"What did Gerrick do?"

"Nothin'. He wasn't even here when we jumped the guy. He didn't know what the dude was talking about."

"What did you guys do?"

"*Dill* (Fuck)...What could we do? He held a gun against Gerrick's head and pulled the hammer back. Gerrick told everyone to stay cool. Someone said the dude's name is Jason Fung."

"Fuck...Jason and I grew up together. He was in jail for murder and just got out. He knows a lot of the guys," I said.

"We didn't know," David said.

I thought to myself, *These guys jumped someone for no reason and look what happens. They could have gotten both Gerrick and Jason killed. Now I'll have to smooth things over between them. I wish I had gotten here before this mess started.*

I used to work out with a guy named Dennis who earned his

Black Belt in karate at a very early age. He had a small role in the action film, "Killer Elite." When the movie was released, a group of us sat through three showings to catch his brief fight scene. While we were at Dennis' house one day, his friend Simon stopped by and we were introduced.

"What's happenin', Simon?" Dennis asked after making the introductions.

"Shit, my younger brother just got jumped at his school by Joe Boys," Simon said. "Jerome got in a fight with one of them, not knowing who the guy's friends were. They found my brother after school and fucked him up bad. They cracked his head open. God, I wanna go kill 'em."

Dennis gave me a funny look but didn't say a word about my association with the gang. I watched them spar and Simon was awesome. He emigrated from Korea and held a third-degree black belt in Tae Kwon Do. Simon was very successful competing nationally in full-contact tournaments. His brother, Jerome, was also a black belt.

After Simon left, Dennis shared with me that they first met after he spotted Simon on a corner in Japantown, defending an elderly woman who was being robbed and attacked by a huge man. By the time Dennis ran over to help, Simon had already knocked the perpetrator unconscious. He seemed like a real nice guy and I felt bad about his brother.

The Joe Boys were quite strong in 1976. In addition to the Wah Chings, we were also up against the Suey Sing Boys, Hop Sing Boys, as well as the John Louie Boys. The Hop Sing Boys called themselves the Tornadoes in order to conceal their Tong affiliation.

Tongs who used kids as soldiers usually maintained some distance from them, especially when arrests occurred. Attorneys' fees were funneled through friends or the young members' families. In the '70s, the Tongs were trying to convince the public that they were legitimate organizations that had moved away from past criminal activities.

There was a group called Cookie Boys comprised of Korean and Japanese-Americans. The gang had two factions. The older guys were led by *Di Bhang* (Big Cookie) and the younger ones headed by *Sai Bhang* (Little Cookie). We had a truce with them for a short time until one of our guys stabbed a Cookie Boy in the face.

On New Year's Eve, 1976, we made a bold statement by marching through Chinatown—over one hundred of us. We met up with about thirty other members on Grant Avenue and Jackson Street, where we established an informal command post. Not a single enemy was in sight. Some of our guys recognized individuals they didn't care for and those unfortunate souls received thorough beatings.

The Cookie Boys met us there about an hour later with twenty of their guys. They looked nervous. Showing up meant pledging their allegiance to us. New Joe Boy members and potential recruits were there as well.

As I stood on the corner acting tough, I felt a tug on the bottom of my jacket. As I turned, a sweet voice said, "Hi, Uncle William." It was Shelna and Marcus, the children of close friends. I looked around and their parents were standing off to the side. My inclination was to ignore them, but they didn't let me off that easily.

"Hey, how are you kids doing?" I finally asked, squatting down.

"Uncle William, what are *you* doing here?" inquired five-year-old Marcus.

"Oh, nothin' much," I replied.

"Why are you just standing around?" Shelna asked. "Are you waiting for someone? Who are all these people? Are they your friends?"

At that point, their mother rescued me from the interrogation by calling for them. It was quite embarrassing. The guys were all laughing at me. I thought to myself, *Yeah, William, you're a real tough gangster...no doubt about it.*

During Chinese New Year's, the Bok Kai (Water God) festival is held in Marysville, 125 miles east of San Francisco. The Hop Sing and Suey Sing Tongs have been established here for many years. The celebration began in 1878 and includes a parade on Saturdays.

The following day is noted as "Bomb Day," when the "Ring Ceremony" takes place. At a scheduled time, participants gather in a designated area of the street. Next, celestial rings—bracelet-size roped hoops wrapped in red ribbon and packaged in explosives—are shot into the air like a bomb. While all rings are considered good luck, numbered ones are deemed to be of higher value. Individuals and merchants traveled from afar to purchase these rings. By tradition, participants fought to claim them.

During the height of the gang war, this ritual was symbolic as members representing the various Tongs were sent in to retrieve the tokens. Victors were unofficially recognized in the Hock Sair Woey (Chinese Underworld) as the fiercest Tong.

It was Chinese New Year's, 1977, and our gang was making plans to attend Bomb Day the following Sunday. Quite a number in our group would be making the trip.

"Come with us, cuz, we know you like to fight. It'll be perfect for you," Carl said.

"Yea, you don't even have to drive. We have plenty of cars already," Peter added.

"Sounds like fun, cuz, but I have tests coming up, I replied."

"Aw, man, you afraid of seeing your father's friends up there?" Tim chided.

"Yeah, right, I'm scared," I replied sarcastically.

They attended Bomb Day and made a strong statement. When the Ring Ceremony began, my friends went unchallenged, claiming every ring. The guys were so intimidating that interested parties were afraid to purchase the rings from them. Even after hearing of the great time they had, I didn't regret staying home. One can only take so much violence.

During my fourth year in college, I dated a fellow student named Jennifer Chow, a bright, sweet girl from Southern California. One Saturday evening, we attended a late movie near Fisherman's Wharf. As we were holding hands and walking to my car just after midnight, we stepped off the curb and were suddenly cut off by four cars. All were occupied by Asian males. They were Wah Chings. I thought, *That's it, I'm as good as dead.*

I was carrying a Bauer .25 automatic pistol in my jacket pocket. Grasping it with my left hand, I released the safety with my thumb.

"Just keep walking, Jen," I whispered.

As each of the cars screeched to a halt, the occupants stormed out and stared me down. I recognized most of them. Next, they glanced over at a figure stepping out from the front vehicle.

It was Michael "Hot Dog" Louie, who had become leader of the Wah Chings. He was either on leave or just released from prison for the torture and murder of Lincoln Louie. I looked him straight in the eye as we passed and calmly walked between two of the cars. I pulled Jennifer into me, preparing to push her out of the line of fire. There's no doubt in my mind that if I made a quick move or started running, it would have set them off.

They must have noticed my car parked and staked it out, hoping to ambush me and the guys. My guardian angel protected me that evening. The other Wah Chings were shocked that Hot Dog permitted me to walk away. Without question, they wanted to start something.

That night, I lay in bed staring at the ceiling. *It would have been my little .25 up against twenty guys packing big heat. What a sorry sight. Even if they didn't shoot me, they could have kidnapped and tortured me like they did to Lincoln. Man, this shit has got to stop. When am I going to learn?*

As the war heated up, Carl and Don's father placed them in private school. Mr. Lew dropped them off and picked them up every day, watching them like a hawk. Matt and Peter acted like bickering Siamese twins—inseparable but always at odds. Chad started to drive and was determined to inherit my '72 Rally Sport Camaro.

Paul Ng gained tremendous respect in the gang. He was rowdy, gutsy and loyal—all desirable traits. Mitch was quiet and laid-back. He lived with his grandmother and attended Washington High School. Tiger, who was originally recruited by Gerrick, was spending more time with us. He was always up to something. He used to take the wheel covers off my car and hold them for ransom. The kid just wanted to sit up front and go cruising with me.

CHAPTER 8.

THE GOLDEN DRAGON MASSACRE

The Golden Dragon Massacre was the worst mass murder in San Francisco's history. The crime threatened the city's sanctity and livelihood. It uncovered the dark side of the Chinese culture.

For more than ten years, beginning at age seven, I peddled illegal fireworks in Chinatown. Trent and I retired after the summer of 1972, as we approached our eighteenth birthdays. The timing was appropriate, as the business had turned real ugly. The Wah Chings started demanding protection money from dealers. On top of that, these gangsters were selling fireworks themselves. You were supposed to pay *and* compete with them as well. Increasing the price to cover the payoffs wasn't prudent because the fei jies undercut everyone's prices.

Kids from the Dhon (East) and Jhong (Middle) Ping Yuen housing projects, half-a-block apart, made up most of the fireworks dealers. Some stood their ground and refused to pay. The gangs counted the number of dealers and demanded a specific amount be collected together. Those who held out placed the burden on others to come up with the money. Arguments and fist-fights broke out among dealers who were friends. The only alternative was to drop out and let the Hock Sair Woey (Chinese Underworld) monopolize the business. But dealers from the projects had to sell off their inventory one way or another to recoup their initial investments.

On May 31, 1977, Ken Louie, the twenty-year-old leader of the Hop Sing Boys, enforcers of the powerful Hop Sing Tong organization, was murdered near his home. Witnesses stated that he was spotted being chased by an Asian youth as he stepped out of his house at two-thirty p.m. in the city's North Beach neighborhood. As the gang leader jumped into his parked car attempting to flee, his killer approached from the passenger side and fired into the vehicle. After Ken was wounded, the assassin reached in through the shattered window and continued blasting away. Most of the dozen shots fired from the Walther automatic hit their mark.

Ken was highly visible in the extortion racket, and there was talk in Chinatown that he recently beat up an old man who was a member of a rival Tong. The bottom line is that many in Chinatown had motive. Still, the police focused their investigation on us—the Joe Boys.

With the fireworks season underway, our gang, with a loose membership of about 150 to 175, negotiated to protect the project dealers during the Fourth of July period, which had skyrocketed into a six-figure business.

On the evening of July 4, the Hock Sair Woey enforcers came to collect their final payoff. Around eight-thirty p.m., the Joe Boys faced-off against the Wah Ching and their allies, the Hop Sing Boys, on Pacific Avenue in front of the projects.

It was Dodge City in Chinatown. Weapons were drawn and gunfire erupted, with gangsters running up and down the street, ducking behind cars and into doorways, blasting at one another. Matt Yuen and Ted Jeung from our side were shot while a Hop Sing Boy named Dave Tam, who was wearing a bullet-proof vest, got hit in the left hand and right arm.

More Joe Boys arrived and surrounded the Jhong Ping Yuen. Tiger and two others approached the stairwell. He opened the door and entered first. As Tiger started up the stairs, he found himself staring into a gun barrel. He turned to run. BANG! Tiger was hit. Shot in the back, he fell forward in the courtyard. As he lay motionless, a bystander rushed to his aid. As Tiger was turned over, blood gushed out from his chest. The bullet had passed through his heart and he bled to death. He was just seventeen.

Our guys took Matt to Harbor Emergency, a community clinic, a few blocks away, where Dave Tam was also treated. Ironically, both were transported to the hospital in the same ambulance. Ted sought help by limping into the police station.

It's a blessing I wasn't with them that night. As I was leaving the house to join the guys, my mother pleaded with me to drive her to my sister's across the bay for their annual summer party. My brother, who had been expected to take her, wasn't able to do it.

"No way," I said. "I have plans and I'm already late."

As I was leaving, the phone rang. It was my sister Mary. "William, please do me a big favor and drive her over here."

That's the reason I never made it to Chinatown. Without a doubt, I would have been with Matt and Tiger when the shootings went down. We were usually together. My guardian angel was watching over me again.

I visited Matt at San Francisco General Hospital the following day. His right arm was completely wrapped and he was in considerable pain. I felt helpless standing there.

"Fuckin' arm is killing me," Matt said. "And my tattoo got fucked up."

"Don't worry about it, man. Bruce can probably fix it up," I replied. "You just need to get some rest." I asked the doctor making rounds to give Matt something for his pain.

"Ah Tiger say jhaw" (Tiger's dead), Matt whispered.

"I know," I said, gently placing my hand on his shoulder.

Matt and I always got along, and I felt like an older brother to him. When we were alone, most of what we talked about didn't even involve the gang or the streets. He had a soft side that touched me.

Others from our group showed up and there was talk about going after Dave Tam, who was recovering in the same hospital. I deterred them, pointing out that Matt could also be targeted during his stay. They agreed but I knew Tim, leader of our group, was getting tired of my peacemaker role. I had previously intervened in a number of situations, cautioning them to consider the ramifications.

Everyone was upset about Tiger. Out of respect for his family, just a few of us attended his funeral. Tiger's mother became hysterical when she saw Tim, forbidding us to enter.

"You killed my son...bring my son back to me," she cried.

No one was surprised that she blamed us for Tiger's death. We just became more bitter.

Tiger had an older brother who initially swore he'd seek revenge. We knew he was just being emotional and nothing would come of it. He was a pretty level-headed guy, and we knew he wasn't going to cross the line, in spite of his grief.

Initially, I thought Gerrick, leader of the other Joe Boy unit, was going to get involved. Tiger was technically recruited by his group, so he had an obligation to seek revenge. But Tiger was with our group that night and our responsibility. Matt and Ted being shot were also considerations.

Matt was released from the hospital within a week and was recovering rapidly. Everyone in Chinatown knew the violence was going to escalate. To make matters worse, soon after Tiger was buried, some of the guys who visited the cemetery reported that the grave sites of Joe Boys were being vandalized.

"Those ass-holes are fucking up the plots and pissing on the headstones," Peter shouted. "What happened to the code, man?"— referring to an unwritten code of honor in the underworld that demanded respect for the dead.

It was now open season and "no-holds barred"—no rules...no honor...no mercy. At stake was the control of Chinatown, independents against the Chinese Underworld and there were scores to settle. The five-year feud had reached a boiling point.

My work-hours increased that summer, so I didn't see much of Tim or the others. Completing my college studies, I was also seeking a full-time job. Perhaps it was an unconscious decision on my part to maintain more distance from them.

Again, my instincts were screaming that somethin' really bad was goin' down. The gangs knew this, the community sensed this and the police suspected this. It wasn't a matter of *if,* but *when,* and what the body count would be.

It was Saturday evening of Labor Day weekend, September 3,

1977. Members of a youth gang were gathered at the home of a tattoo artist in Pacifica, just south of San Francisco. They discussed plans to attack rival gang members during sil yeh, late snack at their regular eatery.

The leader of the group, barely older than the rest, designated three of the youths to be the "hit" team. A four-door sedan had been stolen for this purpose. Weapons which had been stored in a closet were taken out and distributed. The youngest brother of the leader was assigned to be their driver. A second car with additional members was appointed as back-up. To relax, they drank beer and smoked weed.

Later that evening, the telephone rang. The leader answered, turned and announced, *"They're at the Golden Dragon."* The caller also informed them that a cop was outside the restaurant. One of the youths declared that if the cop was still there, he'd be taken out first.

It was two-fifteen a.m. in the Golden Dragon Restaurant, located on Washington Street, west of Grant Avenue. There were two dining sections—the main level was larger and set up with tables, the upper level containing booths and tables.

Members of the Chinese Underworld were seated in separate areas, including Wah Ching boss, Michael "Hot Dog" Louie and Frankie Yee, leader of the Hop Sing Boys. These two groups were allied against the Joe Boys gang, in Chinatown's bloody gang war. Hot Dog and two friends were sitting in a booth in the mezzanine level as other members dined nearby.

Calvin Fong, an honor student at Riordan High School, was sitting in a booth with friends Donald Kwan and Robert Yuen, across from the Wah Ching leader. James Bonanno, a Special Police Patrolman hired by the restaurant, was also in the upper level drinking tea in a booth. Officer Richard Hargens of the SFPD, who normally patrols Chinatown, recognized the gang members. He was moonlighting as security, sitting alone at the bar on the side of the entrance.

Paul Wada, 25, a third-year law student at the University of San Francisco, was entertaining friends from Seattle. After an evening of dancing, they stopped in the Golden Dragon for a late snack. Seated with him on the main level were Denise Louie (no relation to Hot Dog), Wendy Suto and Janice Imanishi. Paul and Francine Novick, regular patrons, were in the same proximity, exchanging pleasantries with waiter Fong Wong.

The two cars from Pacifica pulled up past the restaurant just after two-thirty a.m., Sunday, September 4. They double-parked with the engine idling. Close to seventy-five patrons were inside the popular establishment, one of the few in the neighborhood still serving at that hour. The restaurant's primary owner was Jack Lee, who headed the powerful Hop Sing Tong in San Francisco. Before dashing out of their vehicle, the assault team slipped on stocking masks.

Wayne Yule Yee, one of the people in Hot Dog's booth, looked out toward Washington Street and noticed a man running past the restaurant with a sawed-off shotgun. A second man followed in a coat with a long-barrel shotgun. Then a third man carrying a weapon stopped and peered through the window. Wayne yelled, "Man with a gun" in Cantonese.

As the trio burst through two sets of glass doors, Hot Dog—who was sitting on the outside of the booth—leaped across the aisle, taking cover. The trio paused inside the entrance.

Gunman #1 proceeded into the main level armed with a .45 caliber semiautomatic rifle. Gunman #2 scurried up three steps to the elevated dining area carrying a short-barrel 12-gauge pump-action shotgun. Gunman #3 joined his companion in the upper level brandishing a long-barreled 12-gauge pump-action shotgun. A silver-plated .38 revolver was tucked in his waistband.

Gunman #1 hesitated before he swept the dining area with his rifle barrel in search of his enemies. Suddenly, he began firing. He thought he saw a man reaching for a gun and unloaded a barrage of slugs on him and his companions.

Francine Novick looked up and saw fire coming out of a rifle barrel. Her husband Paul, who was using a chair for cover, yelled, "Get down!" Francine fell on her back behind two tables. As she turned over, a bullet whizzed by her head and into the mouth of the girl behind her.

Gunman #2 unleashed shots in the upper level. Gunman #3 emptied his shotgun, drew his revolver, and continued his assault in the elevated area. There was a continuous sound of shotgun and machine-gun-like blasts for about a minute.

Officers Hargens and Bonanno both drew their weapons from separate positions but neither got off a shot. Finally, the gunfire stopped.

The assailants exited, ignoring a full cash register near the door. Jumping back in their vehicles, both vehicles raced through Waverly Alley past the headquarters of the Hop Sing Tong. They turned east on Clay Street toward the freeway entrance.

They left behind a carnage. By the time Officer Hargens stepped out of the Golden Dragon, the street was deserted. He used Bonanno's radio to call for help and stopped hysterical patrons from leaving the crime scene.

Officers Joseph Arone and his partner Nelson Lum were in their patrol car on Grant Avenue when they noticed a man in another vehicle yelling and waving to get their attention.

"Masked men with guns were running into the Golden Dragon," the man shouted.

The patrol car was slammed into reverse and raced backwards against the one-way traffic. The officers encountered an oncoming car, forcing them to stop. Arone grabbed a shotgun and ran to the corner of Washington and Grant. He took cover behind a car. Peering around, Arone saw Hargens in front of the restaurant yelling into a portable radio.

Officer Arone entered pointing his shotgun to a scene right out of a war movie. Tables, chairs and dishes were overturned in pools of blood. Bodies were lying everywhere. There was a strong smell of gunpowder, and people were huddled and screaming hysterically. Bullet-holes were seen in walls, booths; everywhere. Both shotguns used were loaded with "Double-O" buckshots. Sirens rang louder and louder as additional police and ambulances approached.

By three a.m., the two vehicles carrying the youths had returned to Pacifica, where their leader was anxiously waiting. Their host and his wife were sleeping. They ditched the stolen car and stayed up until dawn discussing the attack, exchanging kudos. They couldn't wait to hear it on the news. They slept only a few hours.

In mid-morning, Tat Chu, another member, arrived at the house. He brought won ton soup which he was instructed to pick up at the Golden Dragon. Part of the restaurant had reopened for business. Tat provided an update of the scene then took away the weapons used in the attack. He dumped them into the water near Kee Joon's restaurant, where he once worked. The expectation was for the tide to carry the bundle out into the bay.

On Sunday morning, September 4, 1977, which was the two-month anniversary of Tiger's murder, I was playing tennis in Golden Gate Park. A man walking onto the next court mentioned news of a big shooting in Chinatown. When I finished my match and got in my car, I turned on the radio, and it was the top story, described as a massacre in Chinatown. The news related that three masked gunmen entered the Golden Dragon Restaurant at approximately two-forty a.m. and immediately began firing at patrons with shotguns and automatic weapons. One person was dead on the scene, two more were DOA (dead upon arrival) at San Francisco General Hospital, and many other victims were in surgery or being treated for their wounds. As I listened to the news, I thought of the guys, especially Tim and Matt. *Damn, could they be involved?* Deep down, I think I knew.

That afternoon, I went over to Carl and Don's house in Chinatown and rang the doorbell. A woman stuck her head out of the third story window and recognized me. After buzzing me in, she directed me to the rooftop deck where her sons were smoking.

The first words out of Don's mouth were, "Your Dad's friend's place got fucked up last night, huh?" I didn't respond, but thought, *Gee, what a strange thing to say. Like it was a direct attack on my father and his friends.* Jack Lee was, in fact, a close friend of my father's.

"You guys know anything?" I asked.

"Nope," Carl responded. "How did you find out?"

"It's all over the news," I said. "That's all they're talking about."

"This is big, man," Don said.

"Hey, William. Did any of those fuck-heads get hit?" Carl asked.

"I don't know. They just said innocent diners were wounded."

We all felt that the media was treating the crime as a major tragedy because victims included tourists.

"You think they'd give a shit if it was just punks who were killed or shot? Hell no!" Don added.

By late evening, two more were reported dead, bringing the total casualties to five dead and eleven wounded. It was being called the worst mass murder in San Francisco's history. Chinese language papers carried the news in every part of the world.

Gunman #1 killed three and wounded at least eight more in the main dining area. The one he feared reaching for a gun was Paul Wada, the law student who was not armed.

Paul was the first shot and he died. His body was riddled with eleven bullets. His friend, Denise Louie, 20, from Seattle was also killed. Wendy Suto, 23, sustained eight to twelve wounds and nearly bled to death. Their remaining companion, Janice Imanishi, 23, was shot in the arm.

Fong Wong, 48, the waiter and father of six, was also killed as he stood near some gang members and the Novicks. Calvin Fong, 18, and Donald Kwan, 20, were killed in the upper level near Officer James Bonanno.

Nine of the eleven wounded were not Chinese and couldn't understand the warning screamed in Cantonese regarding the impending attack. None of the dead or wounded were fei jies. Apparently, street-wise gangsters, including the two leaders, reacted better than the other diners when they came under attack.

For the next week, the front pages of the city's major papers were filled with headlines and coverage of the massacre. By Thursday, the police officially listed our gang as suspects. The mayor also announced a $25,000 reward for information leading to convictions.

Instead of the usual excitement, I was nervous about the possibility my friends could be involved. The scope of this crime pointed to Tim. He was ambitious and was ready to make a statement to the Hock Sair Woey. Although no gang members were hurt, a major assault on a powerful Tong had been carried out.

The following weekend, we were "hit." Mitch and a friend, Cliff Lee from San Jose, were ambushed as they returned early Sunday morning to Mitch's house, where we were known to stay. The killers, who were lying in wait, fired twelve rounds of .38 caliber bullets from two guns as soon as Mitch opened the front door to the building where he lived with his grandma. Cliff was shot in the head and died instantly. Mitch was shot in the chest but somehow managed to crawl up two flights of stairs to the third-floor apartment. The gunmen ran down the street to a waiting car.

Immediately following the shooting, Police Chief Charles Gain announced the formation of the Gang Task Force. The first head of the twenty-man GTF was homicide chief, Lieutenant Dan Murphy, who hailed from a family of police officers. Business folks voiced concerns that the violence may impact tourism in Chinatown and San Francisco.

Mayor George Moscone and other city dignitaries made visits to Chinatown the following weekend, which were covered by the media. The mayor also increased the Golden Dragon reward to $100,000, the maximum allowed under city statute. (The following year, Mayor Moscone along with Supervisor Harvey Milk were gunned down at City Hall. Their killer was former Supervisor Dan White.)

The presumptive retaliation caused me to think that, even if the targets at the Golden Dragon weren't able to identify the gunmen, they were coming after us. I wasn't sure if they went after Mitch because they thought he was involved or simply because he was a Joe Boy. I could have been with Mitch and just as easily killed.

As a Joe Boy, I knew we were all potential targets at any given moment. But we had entered an escalated level of war and I felt extremely vulnerable. In fact, the evening Mitch and Cliff were shot, I was visiting Carl and Don and could have been ambushed there.

I didn't feel safe anywhere. The Hock Sair Woey may have brought in outside hit men. Each time I entered or stepped out of my house, I feared being gunned down. There was more reason than ever to pack at all times. But we also had the police hovering over us. I sensed we were being watched, and it didn't take long for this to be confirmed.

The following Monday, I was at my job with the U.S. Forest Service in the city's financial district. In mid-afternoon, I received a call from my father.

"Son, the police called...they're looking for you."

"Daddy, did they say why they want me?"

"Didn't say, but he said it was urgent. Asked if you had gone to work. I said I didn't know. What have you done?"

"I don't know why they're looking for me. Did he leave a phone number?"

I took the number down and thought for a moment before I called. *Could this be about the Golden Dragon? I know I'm in their gang file.*

I called the number and a man answered, "Homicide Unit."

This is not good.

"Yes, this is William Lee...someone called my house, wanting to speak with me?"

"Hang on."

"This is Inspector Jack Cleary. Are you William Lee?"

"Yes."

"William, I need you to come down to my office as soon as possible. When can you be here?"

"Um, what is this about?" I asked.

"We're investigating a murder," he replied. "You know Jennifer Chow, right?"

"Yes...did something happen to her?"

"We believe she was murdered at school this weekend. We're pretty sure she's the victim and need you to identify the body."

"Oh my God! What happened to her?"

"Let's talk when you get here. When can I expect you?"

"Um, I can be there in forty-five minutes."

"William, when you arrive, just ask for me or Inspector Dave Toschi."

"Okay," I replied.

We confirmed the room number at the Hall of Justice and I left work immediately. But first I needed to go home. I was packing and had to put my gun away. Metal detectors were positioned at every entrance at police headquarters.

On my way there, I thought perhaps it was a mistake. I didn't want to believe Jen may have been murdered. Inspector Dave Toschi is the famous detective who tracked the Zodiac Killer in the 1960s. I distracted myself by thinking about the impending meeting with him. I felt queasy knowing I may have to identify Jen's body.

What if it's really grotesque? I wondered.

When I arrived, Inspector Toschi greeted me. I immediately recognized him from television. In person, he was taller and slimmer. Toschi brought me into an interrogation room. It was cold and bare— a sturdy table and four chairs were positioned in the center.

So this is where they beat the shit out of suspects. Hmm, I don't see any blood. We were joined by Inspector Cleary, who introduced himself. I sensed right away that Toschi was going to play "good cop," and Cleary, the "bad cop."

"When did you see or speak to Jennifer last?" Toschi asked.

"Wow, it's been some time. I haven't seen or spoken to her

in...months."

Both inspectors were staring at me, and following the movements of my hands.

"And where were you Sunday afternoon through the evening?" Toschi asked.

"Let's see, Sunday afternoon...from one o'clock on, I was home."

"Anyone with you?" Cleary asked.

"Yes, my mom...then my dad came home around seven p.m."

"Do you know anyone who would want to hurt Jennifer?" Toschi asked.

"No, not at all. She mentioned a boyfriend."

"We're aware of him," Toschi said.

"Are you sure it is, in fact, Jennifer?" I asked.

"Yes, her roommate identified the body." Toschi replied.

Suddenly, Cleary jumped in and asked, "William, would you be willing to take a lie detector test regarding what you just told us?"

"Gee, I don't know much about those things. Could there be errors?"

"No, it can't be used to incriminate you, just to confirm your statements," Toschi replied.

"In that case, sure," I said. "What happened to Jennifer?"

"We can't discuss specific details during the investigation. Now, where were you Saturday evening?!" Cleary asked, raising his voice.

Oh shit, I thought. "Aah...I was at a friend's house."

"What's the address?!" Cleary demanded.

"I just know it's on Stockton Street, between Clay and Sacramento Streets."

"And what time were you there?" Cleary asked.

Why do they keep asking about Saturday? First they're asking about Sunday, now Saturday. Don't they know when Jen was murdered?

"Approximately eight-thirty p.m. until eleven p.m.," I replied.

At that point, Cleary and Toschi looked at each other and both left the room.

Five minutes later, Cleary returned alone.

"Look!" he shouted. "We know you're in a gang and who your friends are! Why don't you tell me about the Golden Dragon Massacre?!"

"I don't know anything about it," I replied. *They're watching Carl and Don's house,* I thought.

"Now, who else have you seen in that house?"

"Usually it's just Carl and Don," I replied.

Inspector Cleary then left the room again.

He returned after ten minutes and said, "That's it for now. We may need to talk to you again. Do you have any plans that would take you out of town?"

"No..." I replied.

"Okay, just let us know before you do."

What does that mean? Am I restricted? I was tempted to ask but kept quiet. I was nervous just being there and was glad the questioning was over. I felt like I was back at St. Mary's, getting interrogated by Sister Mildred.

From the police station, I went directly to Carl and Don's house.

"They're fucking with me about the Golden Dragon, man! They're watching this place! They knew I was here on Saturday!"

"Whoa!...How did this all happen?" Don asked.

"Remember when I went out with this girl and we ran into Hot Dog. She was murdered at S.F. State. They called my house and made me go down to the Hall of Justice. They asked me where I was on Saturday evening and to tell them everything about the Golden Dragon. They said they knew I was in a gang."

"But you don't know nothin', right?" Carl asked.

"Of course not!" I replied.

"What happened with the girl?" Don asked. "Somebody killed her?"

"They wouldn't tell me anything."

"Who did you talk to down there?" Don asked.

"It was Dave Toschi, the detective who chased the Zodiac Killer...and his partner, some ass hole named Cleary."

"Damn, they're probably outside right now," Carl said. "I wonder how long they've been watching us?"

The next morning, Jen's murder was on the front page of the *Chronicle*. At the time, I was so wrapped up in myself and the gang war that I didn't grieve over Jen's death. I never offered condolences to her family. My only concern was being hassled by the police regarding her murder and the Golden Dragon. There was no real reason to be paranoid, but that didn't stop me from worrying obsessively.

I didn't see Tim for a while, but over the next few weeks I chatted with Matt. He was attending school regularly and getting good grades. It was very subtle, but he seemed different to me. When I heard he was attending church regularly, that basically confirmed it for me.

My instincts told me that he was experiencing remorse but didn't know what to do about it.

Most of the guys thought Matt was just going through an identity crisis and that his interest in religion was temporary. I kept my suspicions to myself.

Mitch was still in critical condition and expected to remain in the hospital for quite some time. We heard his family was making plans to take him back to Hong Kong. It's a shame they didn't yank him back before the massacre.

I noticed some of the guys maintaining a low profile after the massacre. Sure, we were under surveillance, but there seemed to be more to it than that. I don't think I ever saw Tim, Matt and Paul together again. *Was there a dispute or were they purposely avoiding one another?* Gatherings for parties, dances or cruising around came to a halt. It wasn't business as usual. I visited Carl and Don on occasion and they carried on like they normally do. Ah Wah was there regularly and usually arrived alone. His visits were unusual since Carl and Don understood, but didn't speak much Cantonese, while Ah Wah's English was limited. I figured he didn't have anyone else to hang out with.

As time passed, I found myself increasingly curious and theorizing about the massacre, and this nearly proved fatal.

In December, a gang member approached his friends about a

relative named Sam Lee in Hawaii, a connected guy having trouble with rival gangs on the islands. He and his people were impressed with the Golden Dragon raid and wanted to retain the same guys to carry out a "contract." It was worth $5,000 a "hit" plus expenses. Requests for firearms and explosives were also made.

Author's note—the following event was revealed to me by my blood-brothers and is presented as hearsay: A meeting was set up at a hotel in Fisherman's Wharf. Three gang members appeared and during the rendezvous confirmed that they were involved in the famous massacre. In the adjoining room, cameras were rolling and their conversations were being recorded. One of the restaurant gunmen traveled to Hawaii. He accepted the contract and that was also recorded.

Sam Lee was actually Cornell Lee, an agent of the U.S. Treasury's ATF (Bureau of Alcohol, Tobacco and Firearms) based in Hawaii. The sting operation was coordinated with the San Francisco Police.

The second week of March, 1978, a group of us were at Carl and Don's house and someone mentioned a rumor that an arrest on the massacre was imminent. It was one of those someone-talked-to-someone-who-knows-someone-else in the district attorney's office. It didn't faze me, and I didn't get the impression anyone present seemed concerned. I was probably in denial, suspecting but hoping no one from our group was involved, until Arnie Tom was picked up at Galileo on Good Friday, March 24.

I hardly noticed Arnie, who emigrated here in 1976 with his family. Dan Foley of the Gang Task Force had befriended Arnie and picked him up at school, convincing him that he was being driven to a job interview. Their destination was actually the Hall of Justice, where Arnie was charged as a suspect in the massacre. As soon as I heard of the arrest, I knew Tim was behind it.

It was Friday evening in early April when I stopped by Carl and Don's around ten p.m. As soon as I entered, Don asked, "Why are you so late? Matt just left...he was waiting for you, hoping to go out and have dinner or something, just the two of you."

"Where'd he go?" I asked.

"Home maybe. Someone picked him up," Carl said.

"Was there something he wanted to talk to me about?"

"No, he just wanted to get together with you," Don said.

We called Matt's house a few times but couldn't reach him.

We had no idea at the time that Arnie had given a full confession and given up the others after his arrest. The case had been blown wide open.

Matt decided to leave town after Arnie's arrest. He had wanted to see me one last time. I think he wanted to tell me everything—that he was Gunman #1, who killed and wounded diners with the .45 caliber semi-automatic rifle. He would have said that Arnie was the one with the short-barreled pump-action shot-gun, and that Paul Ng was the third gunman, who emptied his shot-gun and used a .38 revolver. Also, that Tim planned everything and his brother Chad was their getaway driver. They used Bruce Romero's house in Pacifica. I think Matt wanted to tell me he did it for Tiger and the bullet he took. He has since accepted God into his life.

The following week, Paul and Chad were arrested and an "all-points-bulletin" issued for Matt, who was described as "usually armed with a gun and considered extremely dangerous." Paul was arrested at a California Youth Authority facility, where he was already serving time for armed robbery. Matt's photo was plastered in newspapers and on television.

With Paul in custody, I became extremely concerned about the manhunt for Matt, afraid that the police and FBI might get trigger-happy when they located him. Part of me wanted to be with Matt so I could look after him. I didn't condone what he did but I still cared about him.

When the police identified the gunmen, I knew they were all minors at the time of the massacre. But there was no doubt in my mind that the District Attorney would prosecute them as adults. I asked myself many times, *Did someone mislead them into thinking their juvenile status would buffer them from serving hard time?*

Peter accompanied Matt in eluding the dragnet. While they were being pursued, I discovered the guys had suspected for some time that an informant existed within our ranks, and they were prepared to "take out" whoever it was. I was at the top of the list.

"They thought it was you, William," Don whispered. "You were acting funny and asking a lot of questions about the Golden Dragon. It was also strange that you were the first one the pigs called in about the massacre. You almost got bumped off, man! But Matt backed you up and said, 'No way, it can't be William!' Aren't you glad it got straightened out?"

I just grinned and kept cool. But I was stirring inside, both angry and scared.

Those fuckers almost killed me by mistake, I thought. What the hell am I doing with them? Stupid me, maybe I did ask too many questions. Enough is enough. Getting hassled by the police is one thing...dealing with the enemy is dangerous enough...but when your own guys think you should be taken out on a hunch, that's insane. What were they going to do after they discovered they killed me by mistake? Say...oops...wrong guy?

That was my wake-up call. The game was coming to an end for me.

The informant turned out to be eighteen-year-old Ah Wah. As an immigrant from China who was affiliated with the Red Guard, he escaped like many others by swimming across the Pearl River into Hong Kong, eventually joining his parents in San Francisco. I recalled seeing him with Tim. He joined us during our march in Chinatown on New Year's, 1976. Ah Wah was very quiet and sensitive, absorbing every comment or ridicule.

In March 1977, he was shot while riding as a passenger in one of our cars involved in a shoot-out on Jackson Street. Ah Wah was seated in the rear when a .357 slug went through the trunk and lodged in his back. Some of the guys noticed that he wasn't given respect in the gang and treated as a "gopher" even after he was shot. When Ah Wah was exposed, there was talk that he had a distant relative in the police department who convinced him to cooperate and claim the $100,000 reward.

One month after the massacre, Ah Wah began working as a police informant and undercover agent, gathering info on the Golden Dragon. He wore a "wire" to obtain evidence against those involved in the massacre. At Galileo, he engaged Arnie in conversation and got him to admit his role, naming others as well. Ah Wah was a key player in the ATF sting operation. It was he who approached the guys and introduced them to Sam Lee.

During the February 1978 Chinese New Year's celebration, Ah Wah shot two fei jies during a confrontation in Portsmouth Square and was arrested a few days later at Peter's house. Peter was taken into custody as an accessory in the Golden Dragon Massacre.

During one of my last visits with Carl and Don, we were discussing Ah Wah's arrest and his role as an informant.

"What's this?" I asked, pointing to a duffel bag on the floor of their bedroom.

"Ah Wah left this here," Carl replied.

"Well, didn't you suspect the thing may be bugged?" I asked.

Don unzipped one compartment and inside were neatly folded white socks on top of other clothing.

"Be careful of getting your prints over everything," I warned.

"Fuck it," Don said.

The next thing you know, someone opened a window and the bag was free-falling through the air, landing three stories down on the pavement. There was little doubt in my mind that a transmitter was hidden in there. The Gang Task Force would eventually disclose that, aided by state and federal authorities, massive files were compiled, weapon purchase records analyzed, suspected gang hangouts photographed, and dozens of surveillance missions conducted. This explained the questioning I endured following Jen's murder, which remains unsolved.

———————

Matt and Peter were driving east on U.S. Highway 50 past Carson City, Nevada, early Sunday morning. Suddenly a small animal darted in front of the car. They slammed on the brakes and swerved to avoid hitting the animal. The engine died and their vehicle came to a stop on the side of the road. They couldn't get the car started again. It's as if fate determined their flight from justice would end right then and there. Around four a.m., a deputy stopped and recognized them from the APB issued. He pretended to call for a tow truck and instead issued a request for back-up. Matt and Peter were arrested without incident. Within hours, Lieutenant Dan Murphy, along with a number of inspectors from the S.F. Police Department, were en route and appeared at their hearing Monday morning. Matt and Peter were eager to return to San Francisco and waived extradition proceedings. When I heard they had been apprehended, I was just glad they were safe.

———————

When Arnie was arrested, he confessed in a fifty-minute taped statement to Inspector Schneider and Patrolman Dan Foley of the GTF. He claimed that others forced him to participate and named thirteen others who were involved. But during his trial, the prosecution produced Ah Wah's secret tape recording, which was ruled admissible. In it, Arnie stated that he would "do in" other Joe Boys who talked to the police about the attack. Arnie was tried as an adult and convicted of five counts of second-degree murder and eleven assault charges.

Before sentencing, his attorney cited the risk of Arnie being in prison with a "snitch jacket," requesting that he be sent to the California Youth Authority. The judge turned down the request and imposed a sentence of twenty-eight years in State Prison. Arnie was paroled in the early '90s.

Paul's first arraignment was also in Juvenile Court. The presiding judge compared the Golden Dragon assault to the 1929 St. Valentine's Day Massacre in Chicago. He couldn't believe that the massacre had been planned and carried out by kids. He cited Paul's previous record and turned his case over to Superior Court.

Due to a change of venue, his trial was held in Fresno, California. His sister Christine was in court every day. Paul was convicted in 1979 of five counts of first-degree murder and eleven counts of assault with a deadly weapon. As of this writing, he is still serving out his sentence.

Tat Chu, who picked up the won ton soup, was convicted of being an accessory to the murders and received a two-year sentence, which was upheld all the way to the California Supreme Court. The weapons bundled and tossed into the water never made it out into the bay. They were dumped at the wrong time, during high tide. Months later, divers easily retrieved them.

Sing Keung Lee, whom we called "Ah Keung," was the driver of the back-up car. He didn't take any chances. He took off before any of us knew he was gone. Ah Keung was indicted as an accessory but never apprehended.

The Yuen brothers had their own ideas about allegiance to the gang. Dale, who was named as an accessory to the crime, received immunity and cooperated with the prosecution. Chad pleaded guilty in Juvenile Court to being the getaway driver and helping Tat to dispose of the weapons. He worked out a plea bargain, assisting police in locating the guns. Chad testified against Tat, as well as Matt, and in return, had twenty-seven charges against him dropped.

Tim, who was not present at the Golden Dragon, initially worked out an agreement with the prosecutor. In exchange for pleading guilty to one count of second-degree murder, eighteen other charges would be dropped. But Superior Court Judge John Westwick refused to accept the deal.

The case, which had been moved to Fresno, was transferred to Santa Barbara due to enormous publicity from Paul's trial. Judge Westwick again presided, and the September 1979 trial ended in a hung jury in. But on March 10, 1980, a second jury found Tim guilty on five counts of first-degree murder, eleven counts of assault with deadly weapons, one count of conspiracy to commit murder and one count of conspiracy to use deadly weapons. He was sentenced to six concurrent life terms and a total of forty-eight years for assault and conspiracy charges. Tim is still in state prison.

Peter, who was arrested with Matt, pleaded guilty in Juvenile Court to stealing the four-door sedan used in the attack. He was sentenced to the California Youth Authority. After his release, he was struck and killed on an expressway where he was walking after his car broke down.

Peter and cars never got along. We used to really "rag" him on his inept driving skills. He wasn't the only fei jie in Chinatown to face the Grim Reaper on the road. Robert Lew, who introduced me to Tim and Matt, was also killed by a passing car on the freeway after abandoning his vehicle. There were others as well.

I remember a gang leader telling me years ago that secret society members were sometimes punished by the gods. It may be death by strangulation, thunder and lightning, or wild dogs.

"Even these days?" I asked.

"Oh yes, in modern times, it would be by automobile!" was his reply.

Matt was labeled the "Chief Gunman" and "Head Dragon Killer" by the DA and media. I had planned to attend his trial but was cautioned against it. Joe Boy members attending were being watched closely. The gang's roster was disclosed and my name was mentioned. It was difficult not being at the trial. I really wanted to see Matt, just to let him know I cared.

The prosecutor described Matt as "The most evil, vicious, ruthless killer that I have encountered in my career." A number of the guys did attend the trial faithfully. Matt's attorney, Bruce Moore, felt the strong presence of the young Asian males sitting behind him. They were scrutinizing every move he made. He shared with me that he approached the case as if he was fighting for his own life.

During the trial, a surgeon was called as an expert witness by the defense to testify about the gunshot wound Matt sustained before the massacre, ostensibly to show that he was not able to hold and accurately fire the weapon. But under cross examination, the physician also stated that, the wound may have left Matt's arm with limited mobility, possibly allowing him to fire the weapon with less recoil and more accuracy. This was not what the defense had expected. Chad also did a big number on Matt and the gang as a witness for the prosecution.

After final arguments, the jury returned with a verdict after brief deliberations. Matt was convicted on five counts of first-degree murder and eleven counts of assault with a deadly weapon.

After the jury reached a verdict, Inspector Schneider of the Gang Task Force claimed to have uncovered plans to free Matt from jail. The information was supposedly obtained from "gangland sources." One plot involved smuggling a gun to Matt so he could shoot his way out of jail. The weapon was to be transported by a jail trustee or pulled up through the window using fishing lines. Another plan called for the abduction of a juror's relative to be held hostage in return for Matt's freedom.

After the judge was notified, he held a secret session in his chambers involving police, prison staff, the prosecutor and defense attorney. Matt was placed under tight security, and special safety measures were taken at jurors' homes.

All of this seemed bizarre to me, and the guys were also shocked. With the gang's workings and membership blown wide open, I couldn't imagine who would be involved in these wild escape plans. Most of us were already paranoid about being arrested for spitting on the sidewalk. At the time, Matt was engrossed in his religion and repentance. I couldn't see him going along with anything so outrageous. My fear was that our enemies hatched this plan in order to incite the judge to pronounce a stiffer sentence for Matt.

The front-page story of "Cops Tell of Plot to Free S.F. Slayer" deterred most of the guys from attending the remaining pre-sentence and sentencing hearings. I prayed   that the sentence would run concurrently. But Matt was given the maximum allowable by law, which would keep him in prison for up to forty-five years. He is still serving out his time.

Ah Wah received a short sentence after pleading guilty to one count of assault for the Portsmouth Square shootings. We assume he collected the $100,000 reward. His whereabouts are unknown.

Michael "Hot Dog" Louie, who had a previous homicide conviction, was found guilty of murder again. This time he received a life sentence for killing an ex-girlfriend.

A number of victims and their families filed a civil suit accusing the restaurant's owners of negligence resulting in the massacre. They charged that the restaurant was a trap with known gang members gathering there on a regular basis. Testimony during the trial included disclosures on the Hop Sing Tong's gambling and extortion operations. The suit was settled out of court.

The Wah Ching, founded in San Francisco, continued to grow. Today it remains one of the most powerful criminal organizations on the West Coast with more than 1,800 members. Chapters exist throughout the U.S.

The Joe Boys disbanded following the Golden Dragon convictions. Joe Fong, Eddie, Cal and the rest of the original members were subsequently paroled.

I put my car up for sale the following year as part of my effort to distance myself from the gangs. The particular model was in demand, yet the car was "marked." Individuals who inquired, immediately recognized or knew of the car's affiliation. They didn't want to be mistaken for a hardcore gangster who had dangerous enemies. Even my friend, Norman, who was the previous owner and cherished that car, wouldn't have anything to do with it. It was eventually sold to a buyer outside the Bay Area.

I felt lucky to have survived my childhood and this gang war. I was ready to put the violence behind me. But this was not the end of it. The "Man" upstairs had other plans for me. My street instincts and survival skills would be summoned again.

PART TWO

CHAPTER 9.

A CHINESE SOAP OPERA

(Much of the dialogue in this chapter has been translated from Cantonese)

As my blood-brothers were being prosecuted, I received my undergraduate degree from San Francisco State University, graduating with honors.

My father, who had continued to gain political muscle in Chinatown, had become one of the most powerful men in the community. Along with Wong Bok Bok, they held top positions in the *Ning Yung* District Association, the most prominent group within the Chinese Six Companies. My father, who served as president or elder in various other influential benevolent associations, was also an elite member in the Kuomintang Nationalist Party.

Our trip to the Orient in 1975 provided a glimpse of his impressive standing in the KMT. Arriving in Taipei, we were greeted by top officials who accompanied us throughout our stay. Every morning, a congressman and escorts picked us up from the hotel in limousines carrying scheduled itineraries.

One day we were taken to Chiang Kai Shek's mausoleum and paid respects to the Generalissimo who had passed away in April. Hundreds of soldiers positioned along the route to the entrance all stood at attention and saluted as we passed. The body lay inside a beautiful marble tomb, at his favorite retreat, which was off-limits to the public.

My father had a private meeting with President Chiang Ching

Kuo, who had succeeded his father as leader of the Republic of China. He presented my father with a scroll, inscribed with his calligraphy. The scripture expressed his appreciation for my father's contributions to the KMT.

By 1978, the KMT faced overt opposition in Chinatowns throughout America. Pro- and anti-Communist rallies were held. Many ended in violent clashes. Ironically, the Wah Chings provided protection for my father. They were labeled KMT Enforcers. In New York, the powerful Ghost Shadows gang was also accused of being directed by the KMT against pro-Communists.

Early one morning, my father received an urgent call, awakening us at about three a.m.

"Principal Chin...someone's set fire to the headquarters! Come quickly!"

We rushed down to the KMT headquarters on Stockton Street, and the front of the building had been torched. Due to the fire department's quick response, damage was limited to the front entrance. My mother naturally panicked, since I often visited my father there.

"You are not to go near the headquarters anymore, son!" she demanded. "It's getting too dangerous!"

"He doesn't need to be afraid," my father shouted. "We can't let those people intimidate us. Son, you stick with me and stand up for what we believe in."

The violence didn't rattle me at all. These people were clubbing one another and vandalizing, which didn't compare to the gunfire I had endured. But I was actually preoccupied with other problems.

At the age of twenty-three, I was anxious to move out of the house. My older siblings were all married, had children and were thriving in their careers.

My mother was threatened by my desire for independence. She used every trick in the book to keep me at home. Being a son, single, and the baby of the family were all strikes against my desire for freedom.

""You haven't married. You're our son...you have no reason to live on your own," she insisted. "You'll be embarrassing us and we'll lose face. What will people think?"

"I need to be my own person," I cried. "You can't control me.".

"I don't think you realize how tough it is out in the world," she said. "You're not strong enough to make it."

"Mommy, I'm tired of your put-downs," I snapped. "You just want me to stay home and take care of you for the rest of your life. But I'm tired of being here. I need my own place...and to do things for myself."

"Well, if it's a place you want, I'll buy you a house," she said. "I'll put your name on the title. We can rent it out—just as long as you keep living here."

"Yeah, right!" I responded sarcastically. "Now you're bribing me to stay here."

"Aiiyah! You're driving me to my grave," she cried. "I'm trying to help you and all you do is disrespect me. I don't know what else I can do. Why are you doing this to me? I don't deserve this. I sacrificed all my life for you."

"Yeah, right!" I screamed. "And you endured all the hardship for me! I ruined your life!"

"You worthless son!" she shouted. "I was stupid for giving birth to you. The worst mistake I made was giving you life!"

As she walked away, I turned and entered my room, slamming the door behind me. Throughout my life, my mother had screamed and dished out nasty remarks. Virtually everything she said rolled off. But her remark about regretting my birth tore into my guts every time. I tried to pretend it didn't bother me, but the pain was sharp. Each time she blurted it, I reflected back to when I was four and lay near death in the hospital. I asked myself, *So this is the person I clung on for? What a chump I was. She never even wanted me!*

My father tried to keep me home as well, but he broached the issue from a slightly different angle.

"Children are supposed to take care of their parents," he insisted. "We brought you into this world and struggled our entire life for you. If you're not here, who will look after us?

My father was also quite dramatic. He'd sigh and his body would slump forward. He'd lower his head and moved it side to side.

"Everything we've done...has been for you," he cried.

Both my parents were skilled in using guilt on their children and complemented each other. They had their own version of Good Cop, Bad Cop.

The desire for independence was a cross-cultural issue for other Chinese-Americans. A number of my friends went through similar difficulties with their parents, often to extremes.

Lucy, a single woman I worked with, struggled for years to move away from her parents. She secretly rented an apartment, furnished it, but didn't dare move in for fear of upsetting her parents. She hid the secret for months. She'd hang out at her own place for a few hours, but always returned to her parents' house before dark. Lucy was thirty years old.

The showdown came one afternoon. She declared her independence and all hell broke loose. She called me from a pay phone, crying hysterically.

"My mother and father tried to tie me up in a chair and lock me in my room," Lucy screamed. "I struggled with them and broke free. When I started running down the stairs, my mother opened the window and shouted at me in Chinese.

"My daughter doesn't care about me anymore! I don't want to live. I'm going to jump!"

"Holy smoke!" I replied. "What did you do?"

"I ran out of the house and covered my ears," she replied. "I just ran down the street as fast as I could. I didn't dare look back. I don't even know if my mother's still alive."

Lucy's mother did everything she could to maintain control over her daughter. She actually leaned out the window for dramatics. In the end, they accepted Lucy's decision to move away. Years later, Lucy shared with me that she was a lesbian. As she made her disclosure, I pictured her mother returning to the window ledge.

I had a relative by marriage who moved away from her family. She was single and had no immediate plans to marry. After she moved out, her parents made her room up to appear occupied.

"Where's Nancy?" friends asked.

"Oh, she's just out for the evening," her parents fibbed.

She became engaged years later. Before the wedding, her parents insisted that she move back home in order for them to "save face."

Most Chinese parents feel shamed if their children won't look after them. In China, it is considered an honor to be the caretaker of your mother and father.

As part of my psychology program in college, students participated in group psychotherapy facilitated by our professors. As we discussed our families, I found strong similarities between traditional Chinese and Jewish mothers. We laughed about how overly protective our parents were and how they tried to manipulate us. We agreed that some of our parents were ingenious in using guilt to control us.

Other classmates were amused and shocked, describing just the opposite. Jane, a young Caucasian woman, shared her experience, which was very enlightening.

"Actually, my parents encouraged me to get out of the house. They recommended colleges out of state and always nurtured my desire to travel. We have a great relationship—my mother and father are quite active and do quite a bit of traveling themselves. They used to kid my brother and I that as soon as we turned eighteen, we'd be kicked out."

I'm sure part of my interest in psychology was a desire to sort out my own personal issues. Labeling our family as "dysfunctional" was trite. It was going to take more than theoretical principles or inkblots to analyze the destructive behavior I engaged in most of my life.

While my father was active in politics and indulged in his vices, my mother didn't have any friends or personal interests. Her family was her life. Raising us became overwhelming for her, but not having us around left a huge void. I felt incredibly guilty about leaving home. Yet, my resentment toward my parents was turning into rage. I knew something had to be done.

So I rented an apartment near Golden Gate Park. During the first year, it was unfurnished except for a bed and dresser. In the bedroom closet, shirts, slacks, suits and ties were all numbered and perfectly hung. Shoes were perfectly aligned. My OCD had progressed from a little box to a large closet.

I visited my parents twice a week for dinner and brought clothes over for my mother to iron. She never knew I re-ironed them when I got home. It was more work for me to get her wrinkles out, but I knew it provided a task that made her feel valued. My mother, more than anyone else I knew, needed a lot of outside reinforcement to feel worthy; getting her to feel good about herself wasn't easy. Her demons were as wicked as they come.

"Hi Mommy, how are you?" I asked, walking into the house.

"Oh good, you're here," she replied. "Don't you have any clothes for me to iron?"

"Oops, I left them in the car." If you're too busy, I can iron them myself."

"No...no. I'm a little tired but I can do it. You need your clothes ironed and I should do it."

When I returned to my apartment, she would call.

"Son, you made it home okay?" she asked.

"Yes, Mommy."

"What are you doing?" she'd ask.

"I'm watching T.V. and cleaning up," I replied.

"Did you put your clothes away?" she asked suspiciously.

"Yes, Mommy, but I have to go now," I insisted.

"You get plenty of sleep now. And don't work too hard."

"Yes, Mommy. Good night."

At times, I was convinced she knew I was ironing my clothes again, which prompted the call. My mother never admitted it, but she had strong psychic abilities. Unfortunately, she also suffered from delusions, which clouded her intuitive gift. My mother reacted to things that had not yet occurred but she was also tormented by voices in her head that frightened and confused her.

1981 was a pivotal year in my life. I started a new job, got married, bought a house, and before the year ended, my son was born.

I met my ex-wife at San Francisco State University in 1980. After graduation, I returned as a guest lecturer in the Asian American Studies program. She was a freshman in one of the classes. When we married, I was twenty-five and she, eighteen.

We took our honeymoon first, exchanged vows at City Hall upon our return, and had the wedding banquet the following month. Somewhat of a backwards sequence, but everything was scheduled around the huge banquet celebration my father hosted for us.

We went along to appease my father. More than seven hundred people attended. Of all places, it was held at the Golden Dragon. Jack Lee, still facing a civil lawsuit stemming from the massacre, and my father were chummier than ever.

My wife and I bit our lips and let my father run the show. Between the two of us, we were allowed forty guests. The celebration was an opportunity for my father to make a political statement. I kowtowed and went along with everything for my father's benefit, and it was an excruciating experience.

The evening of the banquet, as we arrived and entered the restaurant, I thought about my blood brothers who came in gunning for the Wah Chings and Hop Sing Boys. As I stood holding hands with my wife and waited for the elevator, I reflected on my past. *It's really a shame how things turned out* , I said to myself once again. *I would have enjoyed having a number of the guys here tonight, especially Matt, Tiger, Peter, Paul, Eddie, Robert Lew and Cal. I also wish Winston Lew could be celebrating this momentous event with me.* During the bumpy elevator ride up to the third floor, it suddenly dawned on me that my closest childhood friends were either dead or in jail. At that point, my wife let out a scream because I was gripping her hand too tight.

"Is something wrong?" she asked.

"No...I was just day dreaming," I replied.

Both of our families were seated up on the stage at a long table. In the main banquet hall on the third floor, approximately fifty tables were set up, ten chairs per table; the remaining two hundred guests dined on the second floor. All guests registered by signing their names, Chinese or English, on a bright-red, silk banner.

Wong Bok Bok and other bigwigs were seated in front of the stage. Guests arriving realized that seating distance from the stage corresponded with status. Suddenly, table assignments were blatantly ignored and seating tags were switched. Elders from different Tongs and associations decided to use the event to squabble about other issues. Our measly forty guests, assigned near the stage, were being relegated to the second floor. I lost my temper and nearly walked out of the banquet before it even began. Eventually my father and I, along with the elders, moved from table to table in order to halt the seating frenzy.

After bigwigs from various organizations were introduced and umpteen speeches made, Shark Fin soup was served, followed by nine additional dishes including Peking Duck. On each table stood bottles of Remy Cognac and Sparkling Cider. We moved from table to table toasting our guests. I sipped cider; my father, of course, got completely smashed before we even made it to the second floor.

My father's friends and various benevolent groups gave us Lai See, containing large amounts of cash. The money collected covered the cost of the banquet, which Jack Lee discounted considerably. We didn't have enough room in our apartment for the wedding gifts. Food processors were popular at the time. I lost count of how many we received.

Later that year, my father was assaulted near the KMT headquarters. He was walking home alone, climbing the stairs of the Stockton Street Tunnel, when two men attacked him with metal pipes.

I was cooking dinner when the phone rang. When I answered, my father was screaming on the other end.

"Son, come quickly! I'm at the school!" he hollered. "I'm

bleeding...blood is gushing out of me!"

"What?!" I screamed. "Daddy, what happened?"

"Someone tried to kill me! Hurry...just get over here! I don't know if I'm going to make it!"

I hung up the phone and turned to my wife.

"Someone tried to kill my father! He's hurt...he's bleeding...he's at the school. We gotta go!"

So we turned everything off in the kitchen and ran out. After driving a few blocks, I stopped at a phone booth and called for an ambulance. Visualizing my father bleeding to death, I drove to Chinatown like a madman, running through every stop sign and red light. Miraculously, we didn't get in an accident from my reckless driving.

As we approached the entrance, an ambulance with its lights flashing was double-parked in front of the building. I ran to his office, where he was being treated by paramedics. Blood was still oozing out of his scalp, soaking his shirt and suit.

"Who did this to you?" I shouted.

"There were two of them. They hit me with pipes but I fought them off!" he replied. "I kicked them and they ran off!"

"Please stay still," the woman treating him said.

"Fucking bastards!" I screamed. "We need to find them."

My first reaction was to take off and hunt them down. My next thought was to get people over there and conduct a search. I was so enraged that I couldn't see straight. "Are you his son?" the paramedic asked.

"Yes, I am."

"We just received another emergency call," she said. "Your father needs to get to a hospital. Would you be able to get him to Saint Francis Memorial? If so, we'll leave him with you so we can take the other call. He really needs to be checked out and treated."

"Yes, I'll take him right away," I replied.

I was relieved that my father, seventy-three, recovered from the assault, which almost killed him. Although he wasn't able to provide physical descriptions, he assumed the men were out to rob him. I had serious doubts about that.

Any "two-bit" mugger who had him wounded on the ground would have finished what he or they set out to do. No one else was around. Yet they made no attempt to grab his money or jewelry. My father was involved in a lot of controversy in Chinatown during that time and had plenty of enemies. Someone may have been settling an old grudge as well. His womanizing also provided motives. These theories seemed more likely. Fortunately, no other attempts were made on his life.

In October 1984, a journalist named Henry Liu was murdered at his home in Daly City, just south of San Francisco. It didn't take long for rumors to circulate in Chinatown that the killing was reprisal for a critical biography the victim recently wrote on Taiwan President Chiang Ching-Kuo. Gangster-assassins linked to the KMT became the focus of a joint homicide investigation conducted by local police and the FBI.

Political opponents and KMT critics seized the opportunity to launch a PR attack. My father and his associates faced immense pressure brought on by the crime and investigation. My mother became concerned for my father, and for me as well. One Sunday evening over dinner, my father and I quietly sat and listened as my mother rambled on.

"They're saying a lot of bad things about the KMT," she whispered. "People against the party are surfacing everywhere. Communist-sympathizers are showing their true face. Some of your father's old friends are turning on him. It's getting to be dangerous. You don't know who you can trust. Son, not only should you stay away from the headquarters, but you shouldn't even attend public functions with your father."

My mother's behavior, although extreme, wasn't out of the ordinary. What did surprise me was my father's response to her statements. He didn't utter a word. There was no rebuttal. His silence indicated that my parents had discussed the subject beforehand and she was, for all intents and purposes, voicing his concerns.

The following year, top members of the notorious United Bamboo Triad, along with high-ranking military officials of the KMT's intelligence bureau, were tried and convicted for the crime. The topic became another sore subject in our home.

During that period, there were other family crises. My wife and I had separated and we were bickering over the custody of our son. Two of my sisters were also going through divorces, and my brother was contemplating a separation. My parents wanted me to move back home, but I still had enough sense in me to preserve my independence.

The pain of my failed marriage, of feeling rejected, was overwhelming. I was an emotionally immature adult who was accustomed to bullying people—someone used to getting his way, never admitting when he was wrong. Suddenly, my inflated ego had to be scraped off the floor. I had no idea how to pick myself up and move forward.

I turned to a therapist named Ellen Nash, a kind, gentle colleague I met in a psychotherapy training seminar. Together, we started the long, excruciating process of sorting out my life.

One of the first problems we addressed was the increase of recurring violent dreams. An issue since childhood, the nightmares were not only occurring more often, they had intensified.

CHAPTER 10.

THE TAO OF CORPORATE WARFARE

My aspiration since high school, was to work in counseling. After college, I spent time volunteering at San Francisco General Hospital's Psychiatric Emergency Services. The training was expected to lead to a full-time position.

The facility was highly regarded for responding to individuals experiencing severe psychotic episodes. Many patients were brought in by police on code "5150s," involuntary admissions. Those deemed to be a threat to themselves or others were hospitalized for up to seventy-two hours for evaluations. A large number had to be restrained and medicated with anti-psychotic drugs.

For a short time, I was employed as a counselor at a program that assisted clients who were transitioning back into mainstream living after long-term treatments at psychiatric institutions. It was called Assisted Independent Living, located near Haight-Ashbury in San Francisco.

Crisis intervention is something I seem to have a knack for. Keeping a cool head, diffusing volatile situations, and responding effectively under pressure were skills I developed growing up. My instincts fit the profile of your classic "survivor."

I interviewed for a position working at San Francisco Suicide Prevention and considered applying to the FBI with hopes of specializing in hostage negotiations. I continued training in psychotherapy and became involved with a number of organizations, including the Northern California Group Psychotherapy Society and the International Transactional Analysis Association.

Dissatisfied with the compensation in the mental health field, my ambition was redirected to the corporate arena. Soon, I discovered that being a street punk most of my life had serious consequences. My bad attitude and self-righteousness got me into trouble repeatedly.

On several occasions, I literally told my boss to "fuck off" and walked off the job. My inability to resolve conflicts in a civilized manner led to embarrassing situations. Take away my option to resort to violence, and I was just a frightened little boy in a business suit.

I assumed the most brutal people were on the streets. But in the downtown highrises, I encountered individuals who were just as vicious. Their weapons of choice didn't leave one bruised or bleeding. These people attacked by talking behind your back, writing secret memos or delegating work with impossible goals.

In the early 1980s, I was hired by a Fortune 100 company as a recruiter. I barely made it through my first day.

After sitting through the employee orientation session, I was assigned a nice, private office. I unpacked personal belongings including pictures, wall calendar, reference books, rolodex, calculator and files.

After I was introduced around, my boss Doug Freeman took me out for lunch. With a husky built, standing about six-feet-two, he was clean-shaven and wore glasses. He reminded me of my metal shop teacher in high school. He was introverted but not someone you wanted to b.s. Doug and I had a nice chat getting to know one another. I appreciated the fact that he was straight forward and didn't play games. I knew it would always be clear how I stood with him.

Doug described the department, giving a brief description of our co-workers and their functions. When he got around to a manager named Janice Grossman, I sensed contempt in his voice. I recalled meeting Janice during my interview. In her early thirties, she was bright, energetic and attractive. Employed with the company less than two years, she had already been promoted twice.

We talked about our families. When I ordered chocolate mousse for dessert, Doug shared a story about being disciplined as a child— it involved chocolate.

He grew up in a small town with one general store. When he was about ten, Doug stole a candy bar, which the storekeeper witnessed and reported to his mother. When Doug arrived home, his mother broke his piggy bank and marched him down to the store. She made him buy the entire box of chocolate bars. Returning home, she sat Doug down and made him eat the entire box of chocolate. Needless to say, he became ill. Doug said from that day on, he couldn't stand the sight of chocolate.

After lunch, I went off to meetings that had been scheduled for me with my client-groups. I made my way around various buildings and introduced myself. Returning to my office at the end of the day, I noticed a mail cart sitting outside my door. Through the wired mesh, I recognized my belongings.

Everything was scattered in the cart. Files and books were ruffled. Rolodex cards were torn. The battery cover of my calculator was dangling open.

As I peered into the office, it was obvious someone else had moved in. On the far end of the credenza sat a picture. It was Janice Grossman carrying a backpack on a mountain trail.

Obviously, there's been a mistake, I thought. *But why did someone throw my things out like that?*

On the far end of our floor, I saw Carol, my administrative assistant. I approached and asked, "Carol, do you know what's going on?"

"All I know is...first, I was told that my desk was in front of your office," Carol replied. "Then, at about three p.m., Janice came by and declared that she was taking that office and told me her assistant would be sitting where I was at. She was extremely rude. I told her I'd move your things out, but she just went right in and tossed everything out."

"I can't believe that," I replied. "So where's my office supposed to be?"

"I asked around and was told there aren't any offices available at this time," Carol replied. "I don't have anywhere to sit either. I waited around to tell you what happened. I'm going home," she said in disgust.

Suddenly I felt angry and violated. *There's no excuse for this,* I thought. *This is my first day at work. What's going on here?*

I sorted through my things in the cart and tried to tidy up. No one else was around. Doug had already gone home and Janice wasn't anywhere to be found.

Leaving the building, I noticed a line of people waiting to use the automated teller machine next door. Lo and behold, standing at the front of the line was Janice Grossman. I immediately walked up to her.

"Janice, is there some confusion about the office?" I asked calmly.

"There's no confusion," she replied, looking away from me. "You made a mistake. That's my office."

"But I was assigned that office," I replied.

"That doesn't mean anything. I'm taking that office. Welcome to the real world," she said.

"Janice, I don't know what's going on, but I don't appreciate having my things thrown out like that. It wasn't necessary."

Suddenly, she turned and stuck her index finger right up to my face. I noticed a chip on her bright red nail polish.

"Listen!" she shouted. "I am the last person in this company you want to fuck with! You do not want me for an enemy. You are just a little 'shit-peon.' Now get out of my face!"

With that, she walked up to the ATM, turning her back to me. *She* had decided the conversation was over. Like I was a piece of shit not worthy of her time.

My inclination was to grab her by the hair and slam her face against the machine. But I just stood there—dejected. I visualized her head bouncing off the metal and her blood splattering. I couldn't believe what had happened.

This is supposed to be a professional place of business. Why did she talk to me like that? Am I going to let her get away with it? I clenched my fists. *Well, am I? Am I?*

I took a deep breath and went back in the building, into our department. After sitting in a daze for a few minutes, I went to the copy room, picked up an empty box and gathered my belongings.

This isn't worth it, I told myself. *Who needs this? I could fuck her up good but when does it end? I can't resort to violence like a punk for the rest of my life. But I don't deserve to be treated like this, either.*

I went home resolved to the fact that, once again, I was unemployed. I had no intention of showing up or even calling the following day. It wasn't an easy decision. My wife was pregnant and we had no savings.

The next morning, Doug called me at home. It was just after seven-thirty a.m.

"Bill, this is Doug. Carol just told me what happened. I noticed you took your things home. I wanted to reassure you about the office...it's yours. Janice and I have been at odds for some time now and she took it out on you. I apologize for that and will straighten everything out."

"Well, I was more upset with what she said to me outside the building," I said.

After I gave him my version of the run-in we had, Doug became livid.

"I'm going to take care of this right away," he said. "What she said to you is totally unacceptable. Bill, please come in. I want you in my organization. Believe me, Janice's behavior is not indicative of how we treat one another around here."

After a short pause, I responded. "Okay, I'll see you soon, Doug."

Arriving at the office, I was still apprehensive and shaken up about Janice. This was not the best way to start a job. In spite of my Doug's efforts to reassure me, I had serious concerns about the culture there. Yet the one thing that kept going through my head was the story Doug shared with me over lunch about the chocolates. His openness left a deep impression. Obviously, we clicked. He was someone I wanted to work for. It was clear to me that he was trustworthy.

Doug went to his boss as word spread that Janice bullied a new employee. She was ordered to move her things out and apologize. She complied by leaving a pretentious note on my desk.

Watch your back, I told myself. *This isn't over yet. I've got myself an enemy—a wicked 'Dragon Lady.'"*

Many employees in that company had executive sponsors who mentored their careers. I became friends with an executive after supporting his organization and earning his respect.

Al was a retired General from the Army who had an intimidating disposition. Tall and extremely fit, he kept his hair cropped, boot-camp style. He walked with authority—more like marching. Most street thugs would not want to tangle with him.

Al was happily married, had two grown daughters and probably saw me as a son he never had. While we met for lunch on a regular basis, I always insisted on meeting him outside the building. The office politics turned me off and I didn't want to flaunt our friendship. One day, Al came to my rescue when I was set up to take a fall.

Corporate files were audited on a regular basis. The Internal Audit group carried a lot of weight in the company. In extreme cases, their findings resulted in terminations for non-compliance or gross negligence.

My problem started with a telephone call from Sid, a vice president in finance.

"Bill Lee," I answered.

"Bill, this is Sid Cooper. How are you doing this morning?"

"Fine, thanks Sid."

"Bill, I'm sending a résumé down to you of a woman I'm interested in hiring. She recently received her MBA from Stanford. Why don't you do your thing...you know, get her in for interviews, have her fill out the application, do the reference checks, and we'll go from there. I'd like you to take care of this as soon as you can."

"Sure, Sid, I'll call her this afternoon," I replied.

After lunch, I called Stephanie Leigh, the applicant. As I introduced myself and explained the process, her response surprised me.

"But I've already been offered the job and accepted," she said.

"Oh really?" I replied. "So who did you interview with?"

"I met with Sid...that's it."

"Well, did you complete an application?"

"No...there wasn't any mention of an application."

"Hmm...did Sid ask you for references?"

"No," she replied in a defensive tone. "Is there a problem?"

"Well, let me talk to Sid and one of us will get back to you," I replied calmly. "I look forward to speaking with you soon and meeting you. By the way, for my records, would you go over the salary and job title that were offered by Sid?"

I did my best to stay calm, but the whole conversation was quite disturbing.

I immediately called Sid. Another lesson in corporate warfare awaited me.

"Sid, this is Bill Lee. Can I talk to you a minute about Stephanie?"

"Sure," he replied.

"I just got off the phone with her, and the information she shared caught me off guard. She stated that you had already offered the job to her and she had accepted."

"Bill, what's the problem?" Sid asked.

"Well, as you're aware, employment has strict guidelines we must adhere to. We record the dates of when the résumé was received; first interview; subsequent interview; completion of application; references; offer request and authorization. It's our job to ensure the sequence is followed. I'm sorry, but...."

"Look," he interrupted. "I *know* what the procedures are; that's why I called you, remember? Let's not blow this thing out of proportion. Listen carefully to what I expect you to do. Get her application completed, conduct the reference checks and push the paperwork through. Just back-date the information. It's that simple!"

"But this will show up when an audit is done and I'll lose my job," I replied. There was no immediate response. I heard Sid take a deep breath.

"Bill, what you don't understand is, if you don't do what you're told, you're through here anyway. Now call me when you have a start date for her." With that he hung up.

Unfortunately, Doug had transferred to another office months ago. My new manager was Jim Monroe, the complete opposite of Doug. Totally inept, he was your typical "yes" man who changed his tune depending on the rank of the person asking.

The office staff used to stand outside his office giggling when he was on the phone with his wife. His contribution to the conversation was limited to "Yes, dear...yes, dear...whatever you say, dear."

Still, he was my boss, so I went to him and explained my predicament.

"Oh my," Jim responded, as droplets of sweat began forming on his forehead. "This is quite serious. Bill, how do you think we should handle this?"

"I don't know, Jim. That's why I came to you," I replied, looking him square in the eye.

"Hmm, well, I'm glad you did. Uh...let me speak with Louise [the Personnel Director] about this and we'll get back to you."

The next morning, I received a call from Ruth, Sid Cooper's secretary.

"Bill, Sid wanted me to remind you to take care of the paperwork by the end of business today. He said you'd know what he meant by that."

I approached my boss, updating him on the message received from Ruth.

"Louise has been apprised of the situation and is looking into it," Jim replied. "We're going to get back to you soon."

After lunch, I passed Jim's office and his secretary informed me that he was gone for the day. Something about a dental appointment. Louise wasn't around either. She hadn't been seen all afternoon. By three p.m., panic started to set in. My back was up against the wall. There was only one person left for me to turn to. I made the call. After one ring, he answered.

"This is Al."

"Al, it's me. I'm in trouble. I need to see you right away,"

"Sure—you want to come up?" he asked.

"Yes, I'm on my way."

"You're actually coming up to my office? Wow, this must be serious. I'll be here."

The top floor of our building, where the executive offices were located, was called "mahogany row." The few occasions I ventured there, it was *boom*—get the signatures and scram. Everyone got nervous going up there. It was like entering the purely gates.

Stepping out of the elevator, I headed straight down the hall. Al's secretary, Virginia, saw me approaching.

"Well stranger, this is a pleasant surprise," she said with a big smile. "Al's expecting you."

Al was standing just inside the door, with his arms folded across his chest.

"I guess this isn't a social call, huh?" he joked with a big grin. "Come on in and have a seat."

I sat on one of the two chairs in front of his desk. Right away, I noticed a Lai See envelope positioned neatly on the base of a beautiful wood pen stand.

"Gee, this looks familiar," I said.

"Well, I sure hope so. You gave it to me. I keep it here for luck and protection, especially when *you know who* comes in," he said, referring to the Chairman. "So what's going on?"

I explained everything in detail, beginning with the first call from Sid, to the reminder from his secretary, to my management abandoning me.

"Al, do you think Sid is serious? That if I don't do as he says, he'll get me fired?"

"Oh yeah, that's a given," Al replied.

"So I'm screwed either way," I said. "What do you think I can do?"

"There's nothing much you can do," he offered, leaning back in his chair with his hands crossed behind his head. "This is a messy situation. I'm sorry you got caught in it. But Sid does play hard-ball."

"Can you help me?" I asked.

"Of course I will," he replied. "Bill, I've always respected your wish to keep our friendship discreet. But I think I'm going to have to step in on this one."

"I know, Al. I wish it didn't come to this. But what if I didn't have someone like you to turn to?"

"Life isn't fair, my friend. Life just isn't fair. Alright, let's get together for lunch next week. You have a good evening now. And stop worrying."

I rode the elevator back down, not knowing what Al was going to do.

It didn't take long for the answer. An hour later, Sid called.

"Bill Lee," I answered.

"Bill...Bill...Bill," Sid called out over the phone. "How are you doing this afternoon?"

"Fine...," I replied cautiously.

"Listen," he said. "You really shouldn't take me so seriously. About Susan...let me tell you what I think we should do. I wasn't supposed to, but I sent out an offer letter with my signature on it. So, why don't you go ahead and have her fill out the application with the correct date. Conduct the references, and note the date they took place. Then make a note to files, explaining the circumstances for the offer going out without the necessary paperwork, blah...blah...blah, and indicate, 'Per Sid Cooper.' I'll take full responsibility for it. Are you comfortable with that?"

"Yes, thanks Sid."

"Now...you and I don't have a problem, right?"

"Not at all," I replied.

"Great, I'll talk to you soon," he said.

"Alright Sid, so long."

As I was placing the phone down, he spoke up.

"By the way, Bill...how long have you and Al been friends?"

There was silence. I didn't respond.

"Oh...it's not important," he said.

The incident left me feeling unsettled. If Al hadn't intervened, I would have been hung out to dry. I've encountered a new breed of enemies...they include Sid Cooper and Janice Grossman. They're dressed in business attire but fight just as dirty as punks from my old neighborhood. And I thought the streets of Chinatown were rough. Welcome to the corporate jungle, dude.

My co-worker in an adjoining office was experiencing similar frustrations with the office politics and was job-hunting. He continually raved about the high-tech industry and the opportunities in Silicon Valley. At the time, most people thought silicon and silicone were the same material and joked that the industry was "busting" out. I decided to head down to the "Valley" as well. Before l resigned, my spiritual guide had a task for me.

After working late one evening, I was standing at the security desk in the lobby. I recall writing "8:10 p.m." next to my name and under the "time out" column in the log. Suddenly, a loud commotion was heard coming from the elevator banks around the corner. As I made my way over there, I saw a woman crying and screaming as two security officers were restraining her from entering an open elevator. She appeared to be in her early thirties and was well-dressed. To my surprise, she was yelling in Cantonese. Including myself there were only a handful of Asians who worked in the corporate headquarters building. She wasn't wearing a company identification badge.

There was a definite language barrier. The security staff and woman didn't understand a single word being exchanged. Two of San Francisco's finest arrived after receiving a complaint that a woman was attempting to unlawfully enter the premises. Unfortunately, they couldn't communicate with her either. The woman became increasingly upset and was flinging her arms so they handcuffed her. As they were about to take her away, that's when I intervened.

The woman's name was Lily and her husband was an engineer employed with the company. Lily was distraught as a result of uncovering her husband's adulterous affair. Her intention was to commit suicide in his office on the seventh floor. Lily wasn't concerned about being arrested.

"When they release me, I'll just go home and kill myself there," she declared.

After explaining the situation to the police officers, including my background in mental health, I convinced them to transport Lily to the Psych Unit at S.F. General on a "5150" involuntary admission so she could be evaluated for up to seventy two hours. I spoke informally with Lily for approximately thirty minutes encouraging her to get help in dealing with her problems, providing her with the name of a female psychotherapist at the Chinatown Northeast Mental Health Clinic.

About two weeks later, I received a visit from Lily, informing me that she was doing much better. She called her husband, "*mow youn*" (good for nothing), and declared that she was filing for divorce and suing for alimony. Lily sought my advice in garnishing his wages.

I thought, *Good for her.*

It took me a while to get over the fact that the police nearly hauled her off to jail. In all likelihood the authorities would have released her at the station. Thank God they took her to the hospital instead.

CHAPTER 11.
HIGH-TECH WARRIOR

Silicon Valley was very much a mystique in the early 1980s. High-tech companies were perceived as being fast-paced, exciting and not for the faint-at-heart. Employees were a whole different breed. They were perceived as bright and passionate, and threw themselves into their work. Those who didn't put one hundred ten percent into their jobs were labeled "average." And average didn't cut it there. Many employees who relinquished their job titles and took salary cuts going in were rewarded with accelerated promotions, stock options and profit-sharing as the company prospered and went public. Start-ups were still being launched in garages and living rooms.

I joined Advanced Circuits in September 1982. Located in the heart of Silicon Valley, it was *the* premiere high-tech company, headed by a flamboyant CEO.

Founded in 1969, it was the fastest-growing semiconductor company in the world, with ten thousand employees worldwide and over three hundred million dollars in revenue. I accepted a position in their college recruiting department.

Unfortunately, the commute—which was bad to begin with—got worse, as the Valley grew. If you included the few trips I took recruiting at Southern California schools during spring, my car's odometer logged more than forty thousand miles per year.

For someone who had been averse to electronics and computers most of his life, I found myself intrigued with the technology. Many of the engineers were also professors at local universities and taught me the basics of circuit design, manufacturing and application.

The business was extremely competitive, with success measured in nanoseconds and microns. The "book-to-bill" ratio, which tracked new orders against shipped goods, and production yields, which measured viable circuits per silicon wafer, determined the subsistence of our industry.

International Circuit Devices, a start-up firm in Santa Clara, recruited me away from Advanced Circuits in 1984. ICD heard I was disgruntled after being removed from managing the college recruiting department due to a run-in with an executive.

I spent three years at ICD, and it was the most intense job of my career. The commute was long and the hours grueling. Many work weeks totaled eighty hours; most were at least seventy. I lived and breathed ICD, Sunday to Sunday, from morning to night.

Brought in as ICD's Technical Recruiter, I juggled more than a hundred key openings on an ongoing basis—twenty-five of which were deemed "critical," in order to maintain the company's technical edge and financial health.

Managers and executives responsible for hiring were all skilled recruiters who groomed me to become a top corporate headhunter. Many had been CEOs of successful companies in the Valley who were aggressive and predatory in their hiring practices.

We raided our competitors for the best talent, convincing them to give up their titles and salaries. In return, we presented them an opportunity to come in and make a difference in the industry, and a chance to get rich from the stock options. At least ninety percent of the offers I extended were accepted.

I went after Advanced Circuits' best people. Seeking vengeance was still part of my character. The letters from their attorneys to our chairman demanding that I "cease and desist" my predatory raiding were regarded as kudos. And while Silicon Valley's employee turnover rate fluctuated between eighteen and twenty-five percent, the turnover of my hires was less than five percent.

In performing my job, having strong negotiation skills was essential, yet my gift was the ability to read and size people up: trust, honesty, motives, temperament, work ethics, style of management, decision-making, vision, and the ability to respond and produce under pressure. These attributes needed to be assessed in candidates within one or two meetings.

In time, Jack Carson, ICD's Chairman and CEO, would even invite me along to meet potential vendors and business partners, privately soliciting my opinion. I was also adept in dealing with volatile personalities. Coming from the streets and raised in an unsafe family environment, I had developed these skills as a means of survival.

Talent alone wasn't enough to get a candidate hired. I made sure they fit our culture and were stable. Jack Carson would not approve any job offer unless I vouched for the candidate. The hiring managers and I were held accountable for the success or failure of each employee.

Thorough background checks were conducted. I didn't settle for confirmation of job title and dates of employment. Information was extracted smoothly and deliberately. Inquiries were even made on ex-bosses and individuals providing the references. If appropriate, those people were recruited as well. Needless to say, most of the information gathered was not documented due to potential legal liabilities.

Performing my job well required an enormous amount of deceit and lying. I was so driven that what little ethics I had were compromised. The executives, like my father, implied that the end justified the means. I had no qualms about that.

On my one year performance evaluation, I was promoted to Manager and oversaw all executive and international hires. As I had developed close relationships with gang leaders in Chinatown and was my father's honorable son, I became the confidant of Jack Carson.

An intelligent yet condescending man, Jack looked older than his age of fifty. A chain smoker, he defiantly sat under the "No Smoking Allowed" sign in the conference room and puffed away. When he patrolled the halls, employees stepped aside and avoided eye contact with him. One of the gruffest people I'd ever met, Jack and I became the worst bullies in the company. For all intended purposes, we were corporate punks.

The atmosphere was not unlike the environment I grew up in— use of profanity was prevalent; fear was instilled into the work force; everything was about "kicking butt." Individuals were commodities judged by their "value added" to the "cause."

I developed and maintained a "war library" in my office. Binders containing sensitive information on our top twenty-five competitors were alphabetically stacked on a bookshelf next to my desk. Of course, press releases and product data were included, but mostly, the binders held proprietary information: new-product development, organizational charts, venture capital information, corporate strategies, salary and compensation data—all of which made up your usual corporate espionage material. Vendors, consultants, interviewees, disgruntled employees, spouses, friends, relatives—these were our deep-throat sources. Information was power and I desperately sought it to feel important.

All top corporations devote resources for competitive analyses. I attended conferences, trade shows and shareholders' meetings, incognito, to keep abreast of the industry. Company representatives were baited in our conversations. People love to talk about themselves and they unknowingly reveal sensitive information. In my heyday, I even crashed competitors' Christmas parties and picnics for the sole purpose of snooping around. The thought of getting caught and being exposed made it all the more exciting. The undercover name I used was Ron, from my Chinatown peddling days.

There were opportunities to reap profits from advanced knowledge of acquisitions, stock splits or earnings reports. But the thought of facing federal charges for insider trading in the stock market was a strong deterrent. A large number of people solicited me to funnel information through them, but there wasn't anyone I entrusted my life with, which, in my mind, was what the risk of the conspiracy required.

Actually, my forays in the stock market were all disastrous. Beginning at age nineteen, I played the market like it was the biggest casino in the world and got burned badly. Advising friends and associates generated good returns for them, but I self-destructed when it came to my own investments—typical of a compulsive gambler. Fortunately, I didn't succumb to my temptations and misuse the sensitive information I became privy to.

I worked compulsively, which provided an escape from the pain and loneliness I felt when my son wasn't staying with me. At the same time, it was difficult to switch off the job when Eric and I were together. I didn't realize until many years later what really attracted and kept me "fired up" at ICD, which typified your Silicon Valley start-up.

I subconsciously entered another dark world and enlisted in a new war. The "dog-eat-dog," "win-at-any-cost," and " take-no-prisoners" mentality at ICD was how I steadfastly perceived the world. Deep down, I was still an insecure street kid, running around screaming for attention.

The CEO of a competitive company, in a magazine article, declared war in the semiconductor industry. He stated something to the effect of, *We will march into our enemies' villages. Men will be murdered, women raped, and we will dance on the bones of their children.* I was shocked. The man sounded more like a warlord or gang boss than a business leader. Of course, he got my blood boiling.

Being compulsive and highly competitive were traits that, coupled with my dark past, made me a good soldier. I became one of the good ol' boys among company executives. We shared a lot in common—we enjoyed taking risks, lived by our own rules and didn't like to lose. And like young children, we continually sought approval from Jack, our father figure.

One Friday morning, rumor circulated in the company that one of the vice presidents was going to be fired and escorted out by security in the afternoon. By noon, I had spoken with all seven v.p.'s, and every single one of them was convinced that he would be getting axed. Majority were wealthy men who didn't need to work. Their low self-esteem kept them (and me) there.

By the time I left ICD, one of my candidates was abducted, telephone calls were secretly recorded, and death threats were made against me. The company also became entangled in an FBI sting operation and I had to contend with a suicidal manager who barricaded herself in an office. It was the "same old...same old...stuff" all over again.

Prakash Joshi was a circuit designer working in the area of Rad-Hard (Radiation-Hardened) Non-Volatile Memory, a highly sophisticated technology with nuclear applications for the military. ICD leaped into this market, and my job was to recruit from a small handful of gurus in the country involved in this development.

I noticed Prakash's name in a conference program and called his employer after hours, tricking a security guard into divulging his phone extension. Prakash was bright, friendly and straightforward. He was putting in long hours, seven days a week, committed to his project at North Systems. Not what ICD wanted to hear, but his passion made him all the more attractive to us.

He agreed to meet with us out of respect for ICD's reputation. Everyone got along at lunch. Our chief scientists knew, right away, that Prakash was critical in the success of our venture.

Over the next year, we staffed up our NVM group and maintained close contact with Prakash. He received all company press releases, application notes, and invitations to our social functions. The NVM director and I had lunch with Prakash once or twice a month, and we patiently waited for the opportune time to put the "golden handcuffs" on him. I was determined to get my way and earn another star for snagging him.

As I had with other key candidates, a confidential dossier was created on Prakash. I wanted to know what made him tick—his motivations, influences, even vices. Salary information was compiled, including bonus and stock option award dates. For Prakash, the opportunity to be involved in leading-edge technology was more important than money.

I also created a profile of his family and friends—relationship with his boss, mentor, and co-workers. He had no outside interests. His parents resided in India, and he had a younger sister who was entering Cal Berkeley. Prakash reported to a vice president, and their relationship made me nervous. He was a fellow Indian who had emigrated from the same region and had direct ties to the Joshi family.

Finally, Prakash's current project was released and he agreed to join us. I received "congrats" from everyone except Jack. He knew that Prakash's vice president and North Systems would not let him go without a fight.

Prakash and I rehearsed his resignation. I role-played his boss and laid the guilt trip on him, switching from good cop to bad cop, attacking from all angles.

Prakash turned in his resignation on a Monday afternoon. He agreed to call me immediately after speaking with his boss. I waited anxiously at the office but didn't hear from him.

When I returned home around ten p.m., there were messages from Jack Carson and Lance, a vice president, inquiring about Prakash. I informed them that calls to Prakash had not been returned. He finally called a little after eleven p.m.

"Sorry to call you so late, Bill. I just got home," Prakash said.

"How did everything go?" I asked. "Did you resign?"

"Aah...it was murder," he replied. "They kept talking to me...non-stop for hours. My boss wouldn't let me out of his sight. He even followed me to the restroom."

"This is because you turned in your resignation, right?" I asked.

"Oh yes," he replied.

"Did they ask you where you were going?"

"Definitely...but you told me to keep it confidential so I didn't tell them."

"So tell me everything from the beginning," I insisted.

"Wow...where to begin?" Prakash replied. "Let's see, first, my boss said he was shocked and couldn't believe I was even looking for another job. When I told him I wasn't, he asked why I was unhappy. I tried to explain that there was an opportunity to further develop the technology and learn a great deal, but he insisted that I was making a horrible mistake. My co-workers were all looking into my office. They must've been wondering what was going on."

"So your boss stayed with you the whole time in your office?" I asked.

"Till about six thirty," Prakash replied. "Then he wanted to take me to dinner. He even drove me home and said he would pick me up in the morning for work."

"What did he say during dinner?" I asked.

"Let's see...oh yes...he shared that he always regarded me as a son and has done his best to help me in the company. That was difficult to hear. I started to feel bad."

"Prakash, did you discuss your termination date?"

"I tried to, offering to be available after I left to answer questions about the project, but he wouldn't hear of it. He said it was too upsetting to even talk about. Bill, I didn't think it would be this difficult."

"This doesn't surprise me. It's actually going to intensify. But you need to remember what we discussed. Staying there is only going to hold you back. I mean...it's time to move on...you know that. You boss is self-serving and trying to make you feel guilty."

Prakash and I spent close to two hours on the phone. I was simply trying to get him back on course to join us. Extending the offer to him was tantamount to firing the first shot against North Systems. For the remainder of the week, everyone put him through the wringer—his boss, the senior vice president of North Systems, and us.

ICD played "tag team" on Prakash, and I was the "ring leader" calling the shots on our side. Half a dozen managers and executives were directed to call him on a daily basis, pressing him from all angles.

North Systems wasn't going down with a fight. Later in the week, Prakash's boss switched from mentor to victim, pleading for mercy.

"Prakash, I'm in big trouble. If you leave, they're going to shut the division down and I'll be demoted from vice president. I'll probably have

to leave North Systems. My family will really be hurt by this. We come from the same background. You've got to help me out...I'm really worried."

Prakash had been warned about this. "They're going to use guilt, and your boss is going to play the countrymen card," I predicted. But it didn't stop with Prakash.

I started getting strange calls at home. On Wednesday, someone screamed into my answering machine; it sounded Indian. I didn't pay too much attention, until it was repeated the following day. I brought the tape to work and one of our Indian managers confirmed that it contained vulgar language in his native tongue, threatening my life.

In all likelihood, it was Prakash's boss. But how did he connect us; and how did he gain access to my home telephone number? For the time being, the questions remained unanswered.

The following Saturday we had Prakash meet with Jack Carson, and that was our planned finale to net our "big fish." Prakash was, as expected, extremely impressed and flattered by Jack's vision for the NVM group.

In reality, we were manipulating Prakash. While it was strictly business, the successfully outcome of my scheme essentially relied on getting close and gaining the trust of our "mark." Prakash was under the impression that we were fast becoming buddy-buddy, but my motive was to win, pure and simple. I didn't have any problem compromising my morals and ethics to get the job done. I had done worse on the streets.

Late Sunday, we maintained the upper hand. The NVM vice president and I were scheduled to meet Prakash for breakfast, seven a.m. Monday, at a discreet location in Saratoga. He never showed up. I checked my home and office for messages and but there wasn't any word from him.

When I arrived at ICD, approximately eight-thirty, there was a message from Vince Dougherty, North Systems' Vice President of Human Resources. I went straight to Jack's office where Lance, the NVM vice president, was updating our leader on the botched breakfast rendezvous.

"The receptionist handed this to me when I got in this morning," I said, waving a pink message note. After Jack and Lance glanced at it, Jack picked up his phone and placed it down in front of me.

"So let's find out what's going on," he said, getting up from his chair.

After two rings, a woman answered, "Vince Dougherty's office."

"Yes, Vince Dougherty please."

"Who may I say is calling?"

"Bill Lee, from ICD...returning his call," I replied, looking over at Jack.

"One moment, please." I was kept on hold for over a minute. Jack, Lance and I were all standing up. As I shrugged my shoulders, a voice finally came on.

"This is Vince Dougherty. Am I speaking to Bill Lee from ICD?"

"Yes, you are," I replied, sitting down on Jack's chair but immediately getting back up.

"All right," he said. "This is going to be brief. Prakash Joshi will not be meeting you for breakfast this morning nor will he be joining your company. Any calls you make into our company from this day forth will be considered a disruption of our business and will lead to legal action against you and ICD. Have a good day." He then hung up.

I conveyed what was said to Jack and Lance. "This is pretty serious," Lance said. "Looks like they're on to you, Bill."

"It's total bullshit," Jack shouted. "I'm not worried about the legal mumble jumble. It's Prakash that concerns me. Obviously, he told them about the breakfast... and the fact that he didn't meet you this morning is not good."

"What's the next step, Jack?" I asked, moving away from his desk. At that point, Jack's secretary popped her head in to remind him of his nine a.m. meeting. "They're waiting for you in the upstairs conference room, Jack," she said softly.

"Get a hold of him as soon as you can," Jack ordered, staring at me. "In the meantime, you better start looking at the other candidates again 'cause this is looking very shaky."

Prakash could not be reached anywhere. One of our engineers from a satellite office left messages for Prakash at work using a code name that Prakash and I had established for emergencies, but there was no response. As each day passed without communication with him, we knew our grip was slipping.

Four days later, he called me at home. It was late in the evening. What he shared was startling.

"My God, Prakash, where are you?"

"I just returned home, Bill. I'm sorry I didn't call you earlier."

"Where have you been? What happened to you? Are you okay?" I rattled off, without giving him a chance to respond.

"Bill, it started Monday morning when I was about to leave the house to meet you and Lance for breakfast. My boss came by with two men from our security department. They made me go with them."

"Hell, that's kidnapping!" I screamed.

"My boss said he was concerned about me…that I had been under enormous pressure. So they took me to the airport and we boarded a private plane. He said the company was giving me a vacation."

"Yeah, right," I replied sarcastically. "So where did you end up?"

"In La Jolla. It was a very nice resort, but the phone in my room was disconnected. They said they wanted me to relax. Then on Tuesday afternoon the phone was turned on. Late in the afternoon, my parents called from India. My boss had informed them that I was leaving the company. They scolded me for being disrespectful toward him."

"Shit, I can't believe this," I said. "Now, Prakash, how did they find out about our breakfast meeting on Monday?"

"Oh, you're not going to believe this," he said, softening his voice. "They recorded our conversations. Apparently it started after I resigned."

"That's illegal!" I shouted.

"What they told me was that North Systems had received threatening phone calls into the company. So they randomly monitored a number of telephones, one of which happened to be mine. They said over and over that they were just concerned for my well-being."

"So how do you feel right now?" I asked. "You're still committed to us, right?"

"This is very difficult," he replied. "There's something else I need to tell you."

"Yes...?" I asked, anticipating further bad news.

"My sister who will be attending UC Berkeley...North Systems has offered to pay all her expenses, including an apartment...if I agree to stay with the company."

"So this must have been arranged directly with your parents," I replied.

"I think so," Prakash said, innocently. "Oh yes, my parents now insist that I call them in India every day. And one other thing, Bill..."

Now what, I wondered.

"This evening, when we returned from La Jolla, we went straight to my office where my boss was waiting for me." There was silence.

"Prakash, what happened?"

"Bill," he replied in a serious tone, "There was a stock certificate sitting on top of my desk. Attached was a company memo signed by our president authorizing the controller to issue it to me."

"How many shares was it for?" I asked.

"The amount was left blank," he replied. "My boss said the company wanted to show their appreciation for the hard work I put into the project. They said it had nothing to do with my resignation. The stock certificate does not come with any conditions. If I decide to leave, the stock would still be mine. My boss asked me to fill in the blank—can you believe that?"

Actually, I found the whole conversation hard to swallow. *Damn, I thought, Why not write down "one million shares" and high-tail outta there? He can forget all about North Systems and ICD.*

"So did you fill in a number?"

"Uh...it's not important," he replied, dodging the question. "Let's talk about that later."

After we hung up, I called Jack. As I started giving him an update, he cut me off.

"Let's discuss this in the morning," he said, sounding disgusted. This is not good."

Giving Jack bad news was always difficult for me. He wasn't one to say, "you did your best...that's okay" or "there's always next time." His silence and body language conveyed strong disappointment—and failure.

The following day, Jack instructed me to end the pursuit of Prakash.

"But they abducted him!" I pointed out. "And they bugged his phone!"

"Don't you see how this is being orchestrated?!" Jack shouted. "They've covered their asses, man! They justified the trip as R & R [rest & relaxation]; and the alleged telephone threats gave North Systems an excuse to implement security measures...your so-called 'bugs.' Fuck, I wouldn't be surprised if they got the local police or FBI involved. More importantly, did you hear Prakash complaining or pressing charges? HELL NO!

"Now, listen to me!" Jack screamed. "I don't care about any of this. We can buy him out of the stock and match the money for his sister. But this has gone too far...I mean, the guy hasn't even been able to concentrate on his work the last three weeks. He's a basket case. After this is over, if we get him, he'll be useless for who knows how long. They may even go to court and get an injunction slapped on us. Then we'll be paying his salary while he sits around twiddling his thumbs. Enough is enough—as far as I'm concerned, our offer has expired. End of story!"

So we lost a major battle. Prakash stayed at North Systems and got a sweet deal out of it. It was one helluva ride, though.

The whole episode was a big lesson for me. I saw someone get his phone bugged and be abducted; and the people responsible got away with it by lying, making up their own rules and having deep pockets. *So this is how the big boys play...it's really no different than the Chinese Underworld.*

Samir Ayed was an independent consultant whom our CAD (Computer-Aided Design) department contracted with to perform circuit design layout. One afternoon Hal, who managed the department, brought me the paperwork to hire Samir as a regular full-time employee.

I had serious concerns regarding Samir. His work history was spotty—specifically, unexplained gaps between jobs. Each time I inquired, he came up with different responses. He also squirmed when asked about his rapport with ex-bosses and co-workers. Samir seemed to be hiding something.

Hal was sold on Samir and we butted heads over it. I delayed the hire for thirty days, during which time Samir was closely observed. He was an exemplary role model. He arrived early, mentored his co-workers and "brown-nosed" his way to Hal's heart.

Finally, Hal went directly to Jack and complained about me. So the two of us aired it out in the "old man's" office. Jack was amused. He sat there reading a magazine and stroking his cropped beard.

"Bill's holding up a good hire," Hal screamed, pointing a finger at me.

"I don't see why we can't extend him as a consultant and keep an eye on him," I replied. "I have concerns about this guy."

"Yeah, well, he's getting a lot of other job offers," Hal shouted, cocking his chin up. "We're lucky he wants to work with me. He says he can learn a lot from me, and he's impressed with how I've organized the group."

"Well, I'm still not clear on why he wants to go in-house if he's in such great demand as a contractor," I snapped. "I mean, do we know who else he has offers from?"

"He mentioned Precision Logic," Hal replied.

"Right, and I told you Precision Logic has a hiring freeze, so what gives?" I retorted.

Finally Jack intervened and asked me to support Hal. I signed off, "with reservations" next to my signature.

Two weeks after Samir came on as an ICD employee, Hal was in my office whining about him.

"He's like a different person altogether," Hal said. "He's always late, disappears for an hour or two, and questions my authority."

"You have the probationary period to fall back on," I replied. "Start documenting everything."

"What does Jack think of this?" Hal asked.

I was tempted to rub it in and make him squirm, but that would have been cruel.

"Don't try to hide anything or make excuses," I advised. "If the old man says anything, own up to it. He may throw a fit but he'll respect that you did what you thought was best for your department at the time. Right now, he's waiting to see how you're handling the problem. If Samir doesn't straighten out, you'd better get rid of him fast." Hal terminated Samir a week later.

Six weeks later, we got a call from the FBI. After he was hired, Samir had duplicated a computer tape containing the design of ICD's new high-speed memory chip. Subsequently, he and an accomplice contacted SemTech, one of our competitors, offering to sell it for fifty thousand dollars. The company immediately notified authorities.

ICD cooperated in a sting operation. An FBI special agent posed as a representative of SemTech interested in acquiring the tape. At the rendezvous, Samir's accomplice was apprehended as he arrived for the exchange; Samir was under surveillance and simultaneously arrested at his apartment. It appeared that Samir's intent from the outset was to gain access to the tapes which he was restricted from as a contractor.

Hal was embarrassed, Jack went on the war path regarding corporate security, and my credibility went up a notch. I really had no idea Samir was capable of such a sinister plot. The technology of our new design was worth millions.

In 1986, three of ICD's four founders left the company to pursue new ventures. I was flattered that all of them wanted me involved with their start-ups. My network in the industry had become quite vast, which provided plenty of opportunities to work for myself as an independent consultant. The thought of being a "hired gun" was both exciting and scary. There were too many uncertainties. My loyalty to Jack also made leaving difficult.

In May of 1987, after returning from a trip to the Orient, I decided to go for it. Most of the managers and executives in the company weren't surprised when I announced my resignation; they knew my services were in demand outside the company.

My mentor didn't see it that way. Jack's perception of people was black or white—you're either with him one hundred ten percent or against him and regarded as an enemy. In his eyes, I betrayed him. Jack's greatest fear was that I'd turn around and raid ICD like I had done with Advanced Circuits.

I gave him my word that I would never do such a thing, but he didn't believe me. I thought we trusted one another; perhaps we were just fooling ourselves. Our relationship quickly turned hostile.

We had several private meetings to discuss my departure—each time, it turned ugly. No matter how we broached it, emotions took over. Finally, Marshall Cahill, Jack's second-in-command—who was terminally ill and bedridden—got involved, mediating our dispute by telephone. In the end, Jack placed me on a retainer as a consultant with a "no recruit" clause.

Two days later, Marshall passed away. To drag him into this from his deathbed illustrated how self-serving and insane we were. My guilt lasted all of fifteen seconds. I have no idea where my conscience was.

After I left ICD, Jack and I never spoke again; he wouldn't accept any of my phone calls, at work or at home. I felt rejected, like a son choosing to leave home, only to be disowned by his father.

CHAPTER 12.
MASSACRE IN SILICON VALLEY

After I ended my employment at International Circuit Devices, my excitement overrode any fears I had of working for myself. Clients were lined up and offering retainers. All were fresh, start-up companies that needed help setting up their operations and filling key executive positions. Some were seeking board members and additional investors; others were finalizing their office leases and shopping for furniture.

In early August, barely two months into my new venture, a company approached me about a full-time position managing their corporate employment function. Passionate about my business, not to mention the contractual obligations to my clients, I found it was an easy decision—I turned down my suitors.

After Labor Day, I found myself reconsidering the corporate position, discussing it at great length with my psychotherapist, Ellen. My intuition was directing me to this company, called Electromagnetic Systems Laboratories, a defense contractor. I sensed that my presence was required there.

"Ellen, if this were a simple business decision, it'd be easy to turn down. I'm jeopardizing my consulting business by breaching commitments made to my clients. I can't explain it, but I know I'm supposed to be at ESL. The feeling is quite strong."

She replied, "Bill, it's amazing how you've developed the ability to acknowledge your gift. I believe it's a spiritual guidance. You've done wonderful things in your life and it hasn't always been easy for you. The violence that you prevented throughout your life and during other crisis situations you've been involved in was very real. You've taken on the role admirably."

In the end, I made a personal commitment to work at ESL for six months. I told my clients that I would return to consulting full-time within that timeframe.

ESL, founded in 1964, is headquartered in Sunnyvale, California. Acquired by TRW in 1978, the company was located about forty miles south of San Francisco, in the heart of Silicon Valley.

When I joined them, ESL had approximately 2,800 employees and occupied nearly one million square feet of space. Six buildings, designated M1 through M6, accommodated most of the employees. A number of those buildings were constructed of special material, designed to be impenetrable against sound and signal analyzers.

The most sensitive projects were developed in those "tank" buildings. Not even Top Secret clearances enabled access. Authorized personnel required "EBI" (Extensive Background Investigation) clearances. The Department of Defense granted those sparingly and only after excruciating background checks were conducted on applicants as well as their families. In situations where clearances were denied, reasons were not given. That was all classified information.

The words behind ESL's acronym were later changed to Excellence, Service and Leadership. Sales for 1987 were close to $335 million. Bob Kohler, the president, was formerly a director in the Central Intelligence Agency.

The company was involved in research and development

specifically for reconnaissance and communications systems. We're talking radars, antennas, receivers, direction-finding and signal processing. For the military, during that period, playing hide and seek with the enemy was big business. Tom Clancy's *The Hunt for Red October* highlighted the application of that technology. For years, the industry had been simply referred to as the "spook" business.

On the morning of Tuesday, February 16, 1988, I was driving to work, mentally going through my *to do* list for the day. The commute from Daly City, just south of San Francisco, to Sunnyvale took anywhere from an hour to ninety minutes. It was a warm, bright morning in the middle of winter. As I approached Palo Alto, the unofficial north border of Silicon Valley, I was thinking about an uncanny conversation with a co-worker.

A week earlier, a woman in our department mentioned that her grandmother was hospitalized in San Francisco. It wasn't supposed to be anything serious. The next day, I was compelled to speak with her again.

"Victoria, I'm curious about something. When were you going to visit your grandma?"

"Oh, this weekend—probably Saturday. Why do you ask?"

"Well, this may sound strange, but I think you should stop by and see her as soon as you can. I don't know why and I don't mean to alarm you," I said.

"Gee, that's strange," she replied.

Victoria's grandmother was involved in raising her and they

maintained a close relationship. Victoria saw her that evening and they had a nice visit. Grandma passed away the next day. I had no explanation for my premonition.

Crawling along the freeway in traffic, I reminded myself about Chinese New Year, which officially began the following day. We were entering the Year of the Dragon. Most associate it with good fortune. Sons born in that year are blessed with harmony and prosperity. But I distinctly recalled Chinatown friends telling me that certain Dragon Years also represent dark passages and bloodshed.

My thoughts suddenly drifted to the Golden Dragon restaurant massacre. Ten years ago, my blood-brothers were convicted for the mass murder in Chinatown.

I counted my blessings for surviving the gang war. Historians may never understand what the conflict was really about and who was behind it. Unfortunately, they need to, as history does repeat itself; especially when it pertains to the Chinese Underworld.

And then it hit me. My mind was suddenly clear and focused, like I was in a transcendental state. It was another premonition. I knew my reasons for being at ESL would be apparent that day. It was an ominous feeling—my hands turned cold and began trembling. There was some solace in knowing that I was approaching five months at ESL. Miserable in my job since day one, I at least knew my six-month commitment was coming to an end.

Arriving at M5, 1345 Crossman Drive, a two-story building, I parked in the south lot. In addition to my photo ID, the company issued a security card, to be scanned at each entrance. A personal code is punched in to unlock the doors. Exiting the building also requires the security card. Employees carry their cards clipped to their clothing or on a chain around their neck.

I entered my office and glanced at the desk calendar. A line had been drawn across the page blocking out the appointment slots. The day had been set aside for catching up. There was only one interview scheduled for three p.m. The candidate's name was Harry Bowlin.

By mid-morning, I was engrossed in my work, going over projects with my staff. Most of them were in cubicles nearby. I usually stood outside my office and held impromptu brainstorming sessions, peering over the partitions.

Feeling silly, but cautious about some potential tragedy forthcoming, I reluctantly went out for lunch. There sky was clear and the temperature was close to seventy degrees.

Upon my return, I parked in the lot outside the main entrance; it was a shorter distance to my office. It also gave me an opportunity to say hello to Ann Townsley, our receptionist. She and her husband Robert, who worked the swing shift at ESL, were a cute couple. He came in early for her afternoon break and they were usually seen holding hands and strolling, passionately gazing into each other's eyes. You'd never guess they had two teenagers at home.

"Good afternoon, Ann."

"Hello, Bill. I haven't seen you all morning."

"I've been buried in my office. How are you doing?"

"Really good, thanks."

"By the way, I have an applicant coming in this afternoon at three."

"Okay," she replied, grabbing a pen. "I'll make a note of it."

Harry Bowlin entered the north parking lot of ESL on Crossman Drive. He turned off the ignition and checked his watch. It was two forty-five p.m. As he sat and pondered his interview, he noticed a motor-home parked across the way. A burly man in the vehicle sat staring at him. As each minute passed, the man appeared increasingly anxious and agitated. At two fifty-five p.m., Harry stepped out and headed toward the front entrance. Walking away, he felt the man's eyes locked on him.

As soon as Harry was out of sight, the door of the RV opened and the stranger stepped out. To say he looked out of place would be an understatement. If this was a movie set and he was summoned out of the make-up trailer, perhaps it could offer an explanation. But he was no actor, and we were in Sunnyvale, California, which boasted the lowest crime rate per capita in the nation. That distinction was about to be lost.

The guy was a one-man army. His was lugging a 9mm high-powered automatic rifle and two shotguns: one was a pump-action and the other fired repeatedly. Handguns in his possession included a .380 semi-automatic as well as .357 Magnum and .22 caliber revolvers. The pouches on his shooting vest were stocked and every pocket bulged—bullet shells had been stuffed everywhere. Across his chest were bandoleers; he was wearing a headband and ear plugs; one hand was gloved. There was also a buck knife tucked away. All told, he was carrying an arsenal capable of killing everyone in the building, three times over. The layout of M5, where approximately two hundred twenty-five employees worked, was familiar to him. For many years, he held an EBI clearance there. Worst yet, he was also a decorated, expert marksman.

As I stood outside my office, the phone rang.

"This is Bill Lee...."

"Hi Bill, this is Ann. Mr. Bowlin is here to see you."

"Thanks, Ann. I'll be right out."

Opening the door to the lobby, I saw Shirley, one of ESL's security officers, relieving Ann. Robert had arrived for their afternoon break. I introduced myself to the applicant and invited him into my office.

Since it was an exploratory interview, we didn't discuss a specific position in the company. A manager had noted interest in Harry's background and thought it would be worthwhile to meet him to discuss various opportunities. I informed him that after the interview, he might be escorted back to me, or we would get back in touch with him. We spent no more than five minutes together.

As Harry and I strolled across M5's lobby, the drama unfolded. It began with people frantically running down the stairs.

"There's a man with a gun in the building," someone shouted. *Okay,* I thought—*perhaps someone was just displaying a gun to their co-workers. Let's not panic.*

Suddenly—BANG!—a blast echoed. Shirley jumped up and got on the phone. I thought to myself, *Yep, it's gunfire. My visitor—better get him out.* I grabbed Harry, who had fifty pounds on me, by the arm and shoved him out the door.

As we stood outside, about forty feet from the entrance, BANG!—

another shot went off. Employees continued evacuating the building. I assumed that there was only one gunman, since all the shots sounded some distance away.

Glancing around me, I felt that something didn't look right. *Where are my people?* I wondered. *I don't see anyone from my department out here.*

"Harry, stay back. I need to check something out."

"Wait...Bill, what are you doing? Be careful."

As I reached the front entrance, a security officer was standing in the doorway, guiding people out.

"I need to notify the people in my department," I shouted, maneuvering between him and the doorframe.

"Sorry. I can't allow anyone back in!" he countered, blocking me off.

"Well then, I'll stay here and you go in." I replied.

"I've been instructed not to leave this post. Now, move away from the door!" he ordered.

I took a few steps back and moved to the side. I shouted into the lobby, the names of my staff whose desks were just inside the next door.

"PHYLLIS!...YVONNE!...PHYLLIS!...YVONNE!"

No response. The door to our department remained closed. Employees continued running down the stairs, past me and out of the building.

"Someone, please open that door. There are people in there!" I shouted, jumping up and down, peering over the employees running out.

I faintly heard Harry Bowlin in the background, screaming, "Bill!...Bill!" My attention refocused on that security guard.

Somehow, I need to get by him. Going around the building will take too long. I thought about my son, Eric. *Should I do this? Am I going to get killed?* Then it dawned on me that I was at ESL to rescue my co-workers from gunfire. Walking away wasn't an option.

Damn, if only I had a gun. Then I could take the 'punk' gunman out. Why aren't these stupid security guards armed? Shit, is this déjàvu or what? It's all coming back to me now. Well then, let's do it—Chinatown style!

I noted the guard's posture. As soon as his shoulders slanted forward, I knew he was off the heels of his feet. I charged him and shoved him aside with ease. By the time he recovered his balance, I had reached the door leading to my department. *If he comes after me, he'll have to chase me.*

I swung the door open. As I stepped in, it was like switching channels on the television. The scene was surreal. Everyone was working away, oblivious to the danger. I stormed across the area, screaming as loud as I could.

"LISTEN, THERE'S AN EMERGENCY! EVERYONE— LEAVE THE BUILDING NOW! DO NOT PANIC—BUT YOU MUST LEAVE NOW!"

Repeating myself as I proceeded to the far end of the room, eye contact was made with as many people as possible to convince them that I was serious. I back-tracked along the offices on the perimeter, screaming, "EMERGENCY, GET OUTTA HERE!" I swung open as many doors as I could, banging on the ones that were locked.

Most of my co-workers reacted immediately; a few stood staring at me in disbelief. Some reached for their purses and bags. "Leave everything behind! There's no time! Just get out!" I shouted.

Ellie, one of my assistants, was on the phone. As I approached her, she lifted her index finger up, motioning me to wait. I grabbed the receiver from her hand, threw down the phone and screamed, "GET OUT NOW, Ellie!" Yvonne was in the copy room, standing over the machine. I rushed over and ordered her to leave with the others. It was evident that my co-workers were shocked at my behavior.

"What's going on?" Gina, one of our temps asked, unwilling to budge from her seat.

"We don't have time to find out!" I replied, pointing to the door. I almost screamed, "Gun!" and "Shots fired!" but stopped myself. *These people may stampede toward the door and trample one another.*

My co-workers witnessed a side of me that was uncharacteristic. My behavior frightened them. They had no idea a reformed street-punk was attempting to save their lives.

A quick count in my head indicated that thirty to thirty-five employees had left from my area. *Okay, I think everyone's out now.* Just as I ran back out of the building, BANG!—another shot. The blast echoed louder, which indicated that the gunman was moving in our direction. Evacuees instinctively marched south toward M3, the adjacent ESL building.

No big deal, I told myself. *You've had shots fired closer to you.*

As I had done most of my life in violent situations, I suppressed my emotions.

As we ran, I heard a man shout, "It's Farley!"

"You know the employee with the gun?" I asked.

"It's Richard Farley He's an ex-employee. He was fired for harassing Laura Black, an engineer," was the reply.

Just as we approach M3—BANG—another shot went off. All around me, folks reacted to each shot by jumping and picking up their pace.

Shit, is he killing people in there? I wondered. The sequence of shots did not indicate an exchange of gunfire. I knew it was one-way—deliberate. *How do you know these things?* I asked myself. *It's really a shame.*

Next, sirens were heard and police cars zoomed by with lights flashing. Some stopped in front of our building in the middle of the street, while others pulled into the driveways. I'd never been so happy to see the police in my life. The fact that they were armed made it all the better.

Most of the M5 evacuees stopped at M3. I proceeded to the next building, M1, where ESL's executive offices were located.

When I walked into the executive area on the ground floor of M1 at approximately three-twenty p.m., I assumed everyone in my department was out of the building. I saw Terri, my boss, who was the Director of Human Resources, outside the president's office. It was quite chaotic. I sat and watched as managers and executives ran amok, obviously overwhelmed. My objective was to stay out of their way. I didn't remember feeling much of anything. I just couldn't believe the crazy stuff I went through in Chinatown was happening again— and here, of all places.

I was sitting alone when a pregnant woman, quite far along, was directed toward me. She was visibly distressed and my boss asked me to sit with her.

"Why don't you lie down?" I suggested, moving away to make room for her.

"Thanks," she replied, gently easing her body down.

"How are you feeling?" I asked, leaning toward her.

"I think I'm okay," she replied, placing both hands on her abdomen. "I got really scared and started shaking at my desk when I heard what happened."

I wondered why she wasn't on maternity leave yet. Paramedics came by and checked her out; she appeared to be fine.

"Where do you work?" I asked, just to make conversation.

"Over at M6," she answered, without elaborating.

Ooh, she's in one of the tank buildings.

It puzzled me that she as well as others working in buildings further away were just as shaken as those of us in M5, some more so. They reacted as though they had faced the gunman or heard the shots.

I thought about getting up and getting more involved. *They sure could use the help.* People were running around like chickens with their heads cut off. *Naaa...I've done my part getting my co-workers out. I'll just sit tight for now.*

Lillian, the pregnant employee, called her husband, who was on his way to pick her up. She was lucky. Crossman Avenue and most surrounding streets were closed off by the police. Her husband and a few other drivers came in through side roads, picked up employees, and left in the nick of time. Her departure was a relief for me. The thought of her going into labor made me anxious.

Around four-fifteen p.m., we were notified that our area was being completely cordoned off. No one was permitted to come in or leave. Until further notice, we were to remain in the building and away from offices facing north. The police didn't want to take any chances and had to clear the lines of fire from M5, specifically east and south. Farley was essentially holding us all hostage.

The idea of being restricted there caused considerable panic. People wanted to go home; one employee mentioned going to a bar to dowse himself. As for me, I was operating on automatic pilot, essentially unemotional.

Employees continued streaming in. I assumed they had been on our side of the police barricades. As I sat there, I noticed people getting more frantic—the situation was getting worse. People were crying and screaming. Half a dozen counselors were running in different directions tending to employees, prioritizing their trauma. Police were everywhere, and phones were ringing non-stop.

Individuals who were previously assisting others were suddenly sitting in corners, appearing catatonic, waiting for counselors. Individuals who pushed their way into the lobby suddenly demanded to leave the premises. If I was having a nightmare, this would be the part when I'd wake up and count my blessings that it was only a bad dream.

The chaos reminded me of the Psych Unit at San Francisco General on a busy Saturday night. The difference was that the situation at ESL was much more out of control.

"Bill, we need your help," Terri announced, as she approached me. "Bill, this is Susan Barrett, the supervising therapist from El Camino Hospital. I mentioned to Susan that you had some counseling experience and may be able to help."

"Nice to meet you, Bill. I'm glad you're here," she said.

"Likewise," I replied.

Then I looked over and saw Terri approach Bob Kohler, Executive Vice President Lew Franklin, and a police official, who were all standing together. She was pointing at me. That was my cue.

I began speaking with witnesses—anyone in M5 with pertinent information. I took notes on everything. At the same time, I referred individuals to Susan and her counselors. Some required immediate attention, while others were taken to police for statements. My rusty crisis-intervention skills were coming back to me.

This is what we knew so far. Several employees confirmed that one male employee was shot dead in the parking lot. The name Larry Krause was mentioned. We weren't certain how many assailants there were. A significant number of workers were trapped in their offices and throughout the building. Some called Security and the police department for help. Others telephoned relatives or friends directly. Frantic family members and friends of workers began showing up at police barricades. Spouses, siblings, parents, roommates and friends— all of them demanded to get through.

The executive conference room was designated our *family support center.* Family members of employees who were confirmed trapped or injured were directed there.

The television in the room became a point of contention. The families wanted to know what was going on. They wanted to turn on the news. Company officials were initially against it. Susan Barrett and I both felt that if we didn't keep them informed, they would assume the worst in their own minds. We finally switched it on for them. Every network affiliate had interrupted their programs to cover our story.

"GUNMAN KILLS!

EMPLOYEES HELD HOSTAGE!

HIGH-TECH COMPANY UNDER SIEGE!"

News anchors were having a field day. It was also the top story on the national news.

I asked that family members and loved ones be allowed into our area for screening. My staff would determine the status on a case-by-case basis.

"What is the employee's name?"

"What building do they work in?"

"Did they have any reason to be in M5?"

"What room do they work in?"

"What is their telephone extension?"

"Have you had contact with them since three p.m.?

Fortunately, we had access to logs with all the data we needed for confirmation: name, position, location, supervisor, etc. Next, I cross-referenced the information with statements I gathered from employees and the police. Folks who were sent away didn't realize how fortunate they were. The ones I referred to the executive conference room or to the police had legitimate concerns.

Some screamed at me and had to be escorted away. I didn't blame them. They were frightened, which was understandable. The fate of so many was out of our hands.

Witness accounts were startling. Workers were seen running, shot, bleeding, crying, praying, begging, and hiding. Those who saw the gunman stated that he was heavily armed with numerous weapons and plenty of ammunition. He appeared to be shooting randomly. I asked employees to keep all information confidential. My notes were categorized as follows:

EMPLOYEES IN M5 WHO ARE MISSING
EMPLOYEES TRAPPED IN M5 (LAST LOCATION; PHONE EXTENSION)
EMPLOYEES RESCUED OR ESCAPED
WITNESS STATEMENTS
GENERAL NOTES

People were looking over my shoulder, trying to catch glimpses of my yellow note pad. So I wrote the most sensitive information on the last page:

EMPLOYEES SHOT OR HURT
EMPLOYEES TAKEN TO HOSPITALS
EMPLOYEE(S) KILLED!

All statements had to be corroborated. Many witnesses were terrified and this had to be factored in.

Lieutenant John Griffin of the Sunnyvale Public Safety Department and I became teammates. Slightly taller than me and dressed in a tight, dark blue suit, he looked like a former street brawler who had taken a lot of blows around his eyes. I fed him all the leads as soon as we deciphered them. We constantly compared notes. I had come a long way from my days of being hassled by cops and hating them. Still, I felt a bit uneasy around him.

The company's switchboard became overloaded. Reporters were calling and pushing their way into the lobby with their TV cameras. I had to admit that part of me basked in the action and excitement. The drama brought me back to the streets again.

Inquiries from the media were directed to our Communications Manager. TRW, our parent company, was flying a public relations spokesperson up from Southern California to assist us. I did not want any media calls coming into our command center. I was running around like a madman; there wasn't even time to think. Amazingly, everyone seemed to follow my lead.

I organized a hot line to respond to telephone inquiries from family members. We were getting calls from throughout the United States. We had to be sensitive to relatives who were thousands of miles away worried about loved ones. We promised to call them with regular updates throughout the night. Reporters finagled their way into the hot line, pretending to be immediate family, attempting to get a scoop.

We received word that two people arrived at Stanford Medical Center with gunshot wounds, including Laura Black. Both were alive—that's all we knew.

Contact had been made with Richard Farley by police. A negotiator and two other officers were in a small office down the hall with the door shut. They were maintaining phone communications with him. By then, we knew the gunman had no accomplices. Farley was continually hanging up and moving to different phones to avoid detection. The gunman confirmed that some people were shot. He asked about Laura's condition. It was important to him that she live.

"She can't regret this if she doesn't live," Farley said. "I didn't know what to do anymore. So much hit me at once...she cost me a lot."

My impression was that he was rambling on quite a bit. I was hoping he would provide details regarding who he shot and the extent of their injuries. It was nerve-wracking not knowing how it was going to end. The possibility that gunfire might start up again kept me on edge.

Just before seven p.m., Lieutenant Griffin informed me that SWAT team members were going in. I glanced at my notes, which indicated approximately forty people unaccounted for. We had a pretty good idea of Farley's location. The gunman agreed to have some of the wounded on the first floor brought out. But he warned that he would take police out if they tried to capture him.

The plan was to rescue all employees on the first floor. This had to be coordinated with Lieutenant Ruben Grijalva, the negotiator, so he'd occupy Farley on the phone. We were almost certain Farley knew employees were hiding nearby, and he was essentially holding them hostage.

I was hanging by Lieutenant Griffin's coattail. He had his walkie-talkie pressed against the side of his face like an appendage. I could hear people conversing—excited voices speaking in short phrases, mixed with loud static noises.

We waited...and waited...and waited.

Lieutenant Griffin turned abruptly. "We got 'em. They're on their way," he shouted, stepping away from me. "Bring them in the back entrance," he screamed into the radio. "Okay, Bill, let's go." I suddenly experienced a head rush—it was quite exhilarating. The sensation was equivalent to gambling and jumping across rooftops in Chinatown.

We cleared a route for the rescued employees. After a few minutes, about a dozen men and women walked in surrounded by the SWAT team. One woman appeared to be pretty shaken up and was taken away by paramedics. Claps and cheers greeted them. Four responded by pumping their fists into the air. They were moving independently of one another. All were maintaining their composure.

As they were led into the room, I politely asked each one's name. I informed a number of them that loved ones were waiting. I also made sure everyone knew we had counselors available.

The police spent an average of thirty minutes with each person. They wanted to gather information while it was still fresh in the employees' minds. Investigators were desperately seeking information on Farley, victims and others trapped on the second floor. Statements from rescued employees corroborated earlier witness accounts that Farley basically shot at anyone who stood in his path. I matched their names with the list I had and grouped it with people who were waiting for them.

As I entered the conference room, everyone looked up at me.

Instead of making a general announcement, I approached people individually. We directed one man to the hospital, where his wife was taken as a precaution. I hated the fact that I couldn't give everyone positive news. As each person got up from the conference table to reunite with loved ones, they offered prayers and support to others remaining, encouraging them to keep their hopes up. Most exchanged phone numbers and promised to stay in contact. It was touching yet difficult for me to witness. I knew we would not be able to reunite all of the family members with the missing employees. Some will be devastated and have their lives torn apart. I was continually praying for a miracle—that Larry Krause was the only one dead.

The reunions were very emotional. Lots of hugs and tears. Most people left immediately with their loved ones. I saw one employee break down as soon as she left the building. A young woman named Lauren Wilson, who worked in the company with her husband, Buddy, was nervously pacing back and forth outside the conference room, awaiting word on him.

A small group of rescued employees walked out of the police interviews, and their responses shocked me. Three of them, including a middle-aged woman, wanted to go back in and get Farley.

"Give me a gun and I'll take care of the bastard myself!" she shouted angrily.

Others supported the idea, and from their demeanor, I knew they were serious. The look in their eyes reminded me of enraged gang members I grew up around. They weren't interested in talking to counselors. Revenge was the only therapy they desired.

A dozen names were checked off my list. *Great,* I thought...*but twenty-five remain.* I found myself obsessively recounting the number of names on my list, praying that the number would magically dwindle with each count. Silly me.

Just as we were completing the reunions, another situation came up. Leslie, one of my subordinates "manning" the hot line, sent for me. It was urgent. As I entered, she covered the handset and looked up at me.

"Bill, I have an employee on the line. He's at home and says news reports on the radio were announcing the locations where employees are trapped...including room numbers."

"No way...I can't believe that. Is he certain?"

"Yes, I asked him repeatedly," she replied.

"What station is it, Leslie?"

Right then, Terri came in and pulled me away. I made a scribbling motion to Leslie and pointed at myself, requesting her to write down and bring me the information. She nodded to me, indicating that she understood.

Terri and I spoke at the same time. I wanted to report the news problem—she had something important to tell me as well.

"Terri..."

"Bill..."

"Listen to me, Bill! We have news stations reporting where employees are trapped in M5."

"I know...that's what Leslie just told me. It's on the radio."

"We're working with the police to stop the reports," Terri said, turning away from me.

"Okay, in the meantime, I'll find out if anyone keeps a radio at their desk that Farley may have access to," I replied.

As Terri took off in one direction, I headed the other way then realized I was going the wrong way. *Come on, man, get yourself together. Those poor people in M5; they're sitting ducks.*

Apparently, news stations were listening in on police scans and picked up vital information regarding trapped employees. Reporting it to the public was totally irresponsible. Reporters were also hanging around the lobby and parking lot of M1 gathering data on people still in M5. If that weren't enough, they obtained phone extensions and were direct-dialing into offices in hopes of conducting live interviews with trapped individuals.

The cat-and-mouse game with Farley had become quite complex. Besides tracking his location, we had to keep him away from specific areas where people were hiding.

Trapped employees had enough to deal with without having their room numbers broadcast to the public. I was going to suggest leaking false information to the press in hopes of throwing Farley off, but employees were scattered everywhere. We couldn't risk unintentionally directing Farley to people hiding out.

There were three employees who assisted me in the lobby. They weren't officially chosen. As the hours passed, they offered to help and got things done. Their names were Michelle, Tony and Kerry. I believe all were engineers in Laura Black's department. They were invaluable in gathering information for me and communicating to other employees as requested. I asked them to spread the word that ESL folks were not to speak with the media. Also, to check with all the people in the area and report back with information on whether

Farley may have had access to a radio upstairs in M5.

We also needed to tell people to stay off the phones. The numbers on the secretaries' consoles lit up when the phones were in use. Farley would be alerted to people in their offices. We knew Farley was searching the area, and we had to stay a step ahead of him. At times, I felt it was personal—between Farley and me; he represented my old enemies.

We were informed that Lieutenant Grijalva's strategy was to wear Farley out. The sentiment among many of the employees was that they hoped the standoff would end with Farley being carried out in a body bag.

When this ordeal began, my initial reaction was anger. But as the hours passed, I just wanted the crisis to end. Farley didn't matter to me anymore. But I had a bad feeling about the number of victims in our building. Unfortunately, my intuition was pretty accurate when it came to these things. In the old days, when I was informed that one of my blood-brothers had been shot, my gut reaction told me if he was still alive.

All the talk of the media and the television in the conference room made me think of my son Eric. He was with his mother. I knew he watched the news occasionally and may have heard about this. I called home and retrieved my messages. Friends had called, concerned about my welfare. My good friend Jeanine, who lives in Oregon, left a message, virtually in tears. She demanded that I call her no matter how late it was. She just needed to know I was okay. But first, I needed to talk to my son.

The phone rang and my ex-wife answered.

"Hi, it's me. Is Eric there with you?"

"Yeah, he's right here."

"Do you by chance have the news turned on or have you heard what happened?"

"No, what's going on?" she asked.

"Well, there was a shooting at work and the gunman is still inside...but I'm alright."

"Gee, that's terrible," she said.

"Would you please put Eric on."

"Dad? What's the matter?"

"Hi, Buddy. Daddy's at work and I'm fine. You might hear that there's a man with a gun at ESL. He's in another building. I just didn't want you to worry, okay?"

"Dad, come home."

"Buddy, I'll call you later or tomorrow, alright? I have to go now. I love you."

"Love you , Dad."

Next, I called my therapist Ellen. I left her a message summarizing what was going on adding that I needed to talk to her when I got home. I just didn't know what time it would be.

Michelle informed me that a number of people did have radios in their offices. In fact, one location she described made my stomach turn; it was the area Farley had recently called Lieutenant Grijalva from.

Man, this is not good. At least we aren't hearing any more gunfire. And as long as the lieutenant keeps Farley on the phone, he'll be occupied...hopefully.

My mind was racing in different directions. I began praying...*God, please help these people; God, please help them.* In between, I was chanting—*Farley, kill yourself—Farley, kill yourself...now!*

Around seven-thirty p.m., boxes full of sandwiches and soft drinks were brought into the command center. Food was the last thing on my mind. The wrappers had Togo's written on them, a popular deli located nearby.

"Bill, he's asking for food," Lieutenant Griffin announced as he rushed by.

Hmm, can we spike the food to knock him out? I wondered. *Can one of the sharpshooters "take him out" when the food is delivered or picked up?*

Farley had specifically asked for a Togo's #26, which was a turkey, ham & cheese sandwich. He also wanted a Diet Pepsi. The deli filled the special order and delivered it directly to one of Grijalva's men.

Some time around eight p.m., after hours of discussing his hobbies, attorneys, jail, his mother, Laura, ESL employees and suicide, Farley and Lieutenant Grijalva discussed the best way for him to give himself up. Informing Rich that his sandwich and soda had arrived, Grijalva prodded Farley to surrender, pointing out that the ice was melting.

Finally, at eight-thirty p.m., five and a half hours after he first entered M5, Richard Farley announced that he was coming out. He walked backwards, a step at a time, down the front lobby stairs with his arms raised. Seventy-five police and rescue personnel surrounding M5 greeted him. Along with the Togo's #26 and Diet Pepsi, Lieutenant Grijalva whisked him away.

"Farley surrendered...we took him away," the police captain announced. "We're moving in...but with caution. The place may be booby-trapped."

So they did take him alive, I thought. *At least the standoff is over. Let's hope he didn't "rig" the building. We've got to notify the remaining employees in there to stay put and wait for the police. We can't let our guard down yet.*

For the first thirty minutes, nothing really changed. We weren't about to rush back to our offices. I wondered if my car was damaged from gunfire. There were cautious sighs of relief from friends and families. The same questions were continually asked: "Bill, what can you tell us?...When will we know?" Bob Kohler and Lew Franklin spent a great deal of time in the conference room, and I admired them for that.

"I'm going over there," Griffin said. "The building is still cordoned off and all of you must stay away." When he said it, he looked directly at me, and I became defensive. *What's he looking at me for? I don't have any desire to get myself blown up.*

By nine-thirty p.m., police completed their sweep of the building. Employees were discovered hiding under desks, and above, in the ceilings. Upon seeing the SWAT team, some were paranoid and demanded to see identification. As we suspected and feared, Farley had a radio turned on where he was hiding out. It appeared he attempted to follow the news reports as he conversed with Grijalva.

The Lieutenant did an excellent job distracting him from the workers hiding out.

The trapped employees trickled in one by one around nine forty-five p.m. Police didn't detain them very long. I approached a few and introduced myself, while others were led to me. Some were quiet—others spoke non-stop. A few were compelled to share their traumatic experiences—crawling in the ceilings, witnessing co-workers gunned down. We advised them to keep their statements confidential for the time being. Everything needed to be confirmed, and too many things were going on at once. With the details I had, there was enough information for me to conclude that at least three of my co-workers were dead.

Lieutenant Griffin returned and we went over names of employees in the last group rescued. Excluding the injured, there were sixteen of them. At that point, Larry Krause was the only one confirmed dead. That left me with eight workers unaccounted for. Messages left at their homes had not been returned.

At ten-thirty p.m., a half-dozen family members remained in the conference room. The police notified us that the front parking lot would remain cordoned off through the night. It was designated as part of the crime scene. My car was impounded in front of the building. ESL summoned taxi-cabs for anyone needing them.

Quite a number of employees who dashed out of M5 found themselves without car and house keys. Impromptu lodging accommodations were made among co-workers, while others were sent to motels. Lines of Sunnyvale cabs were pulling up to the building, along with cars of families, roommates and friends.

Griffin walked into the command center and made a beeline for me.

"Bill, look at me," he said. "Now, I need you to keep calm about what I'm going to tell you. You're the first one we're sharing this with...are you with me?"

"Yes!...Yes!" I assured him.

"We have seven dead," he whispered.

"Seven," I repeated with a straight face.

"Yes...that's been confirmed by the coroner."

Seven?!...Seven?!...My God...I thought three was bad enough. That means there's probably no hope for the remaining family members waiting. What am I going to do?

"I need you to make a copy of your list for me right away. We're working with the coroner to identify the bodies," Griffin said.

"Didn't they have their badges on?" I asked.

"I understand some of the badges on the bodies were shot up. A few didn't have any identification on them. We're trying to piece everything together. It's going to take time."

Walking into the copy room, I noticed that my hands were shaking. I couldn't line up the edge of the paper against the glass of the machine. On my list were names—each representing a real person—individuals perhaps no longer alive.

I continued moving about, pretending nothing had changed. For me, dealing with the violence and chaos was trivial compared to this.

Around one a.m., we received a list confirming the murder victims. Bob Kohler requested that ESL, instead of the police, notify victims' families. First he had to get consensus from law enforcement officials. Next we needed to get into each of the victims' personnel files to confirm who they designated to be contacted in an emergency.

Anxious relatives were sent home, with assurances that they would be called as soon as possible. Counselors advised each to have someone stay with them. Bob eventually received authorization to handle the notifications. I know he regarded ESL employees as his family and wanted to do whatever he could. I gave him a lot of credit for his role—not only did he make stellar reports in front of the employees when called for, but he was willing to take the heat in times of trouble as well.

It was announced that M5 would be closed for at least two days. Employees in our building were excused from their jobs. Many indicated that they wanted to come in and would report to other buildings to support co-workers. I was told to report back by seven-thirty a.m. the next morning. One M5 employee was still missing.

"Bill, a few of us are checking into the Travelodge down the street. Would you like a room and remain in the area?" Terri asked. "I'm sure you can have overnight laundry service."

"No, thanks. Although it's quite a distance, I'd like to go home."

It was just after two a.m. when I stepped into the cab. I was physically and emotionally drained. I didn't realize how sore my back and legs were until I settled in the back seat.

The driver was sensitive to the ordeal and attempted to make conversation with me. He brought up every topic except the massacre. He seemed concerned when I didn't speak or respond to him. I could see him continually checking on me through the rear-view mirror. The guy was quite considerate. The ride took forty-five minutes. Finally we reached my townhouse. He grabbed the pen tucked behind his ear and handed it to me. I signed the voucher.

"Hey, man, you gonna be okay?" he asked.

Looking away from him, I mumbled, "Yeah, I'll be fine...thanks."

I stepped out of the cab, slammed the door and hobbled to my townhouse. As I entered, there was comfort in the darkness. I stumbled into my living room. Moonlight entering through one window illuminated portions of the room. I switched on the gas fireplace, knelt down on the floor and just sat there.

The past twelve hours caught up with me. The faces of the victims' families were locked in my head. Just trying to imagine what they were going through was too much to handle. Suddenly I broke down crying...uncontrollably. Was the grieving for my co-workers or was it sorrow for myself? I had no idea, perhaps both. My emotions were overwhelming. They unleashed the first moment I was alone. I lay there bawling my eyes out until I dozed off.

After a brief period, I awoke, congested from my tears. I reached for the telephone. I was barely able to see in the dark, but a tiny red light was flickering on my answering machine, indicating messages stored. The first was from my sister.

"Hi, William, it's Mary. I heard on the news of a big shooting in Silicon Valley. I'm not sure if you work close to where it happened, but I hope you weren't affected by it. Take care."

How ironic, I thought. She must have missed the name of the company on the news.

The second message perked me up. "Bill, this is Ellen. I'm glad you called. I heard the news about the same time I received your message. Feel free to call me at home whenever you get in. Don't worry about the time."

I skipped through the remaining messages and called Ellen. It must have been around three-thirty a.m. Yet she was awake and knew it had to be me.

"Hi...Bill?"

"Yes, Ellen...it's me."

"It's so good to hear your voice. My, my, what you must have been through. How are you holding up?" she asked.

"Hmm, I really don't know what I'm feeling right now. This has been a grueling experience. You think this is what the guy upstairs had in mind for me?"

"It does appear that way, doesn't it...?" she replied.

After briefly describing the ordeal, I shared the most difficult aspects of the experience—dealing with the victims' families. The look of their pain and devastation was burnt into my memory.

"Bill, you really need to focus on what you did for everyone. Going back in and saving your co-workers; organizing the efforts; assisting the families. The employees and relatives benefited tremendously from your presence there. Based on what you described, it sounds like you performed miraculously well. I know this was very difficult for you."

"Ellen, I keep feeling like I should have done more. Why did so many people have to die?"

"Bill, you're not responsible for what the gunman did. Right now, it's important to be gentle with yourself and take care of your needs. You've been through a lot."

Of course, she was right. Ellen was a great therapist and knew me better than anyone. At that moment, she helped make sense of the trauma and recognized how vulnerable I was. My tendency was to feel guilty and beat myself up for not doing enough. Ellen offered the best validation by reminding me to nurture myself.

After we hung up, I debated about going to bed. It was already four a.m. At most, I would catch two hours of sleep. Although exhausted, I was also afraid of having nightmares about the massacre. I collapsed on the bed, fully clothed, and conked out. My last thought was that seven of my co-workers were gone, forever. They were human beings—someone's daughter, son, wife, husband and sibling.

———

At six forty-five a.m. the following morning, I grabbed the keys to my second car and headed back to work. The morning news on television reported seven dead at ESL—five men and two women. Four other employees were injured. Police had not released any names pending notification of families. I already knew the task had been completed a few hours earlier. Laura Black, Richard Farley and ESL all became household names overnight.

Approaching the freeway, I reminded myself to return phone calls to people who called concerned about my welfare. Jeanine in Oregon was at the top of my list.

A cassette containing soothing jazz music was inserted for my commute.

Then, for the second consecutive day, I had a spiritual experience. I didn't want anything to do with it, but it was very powerful—so intense that I was able to identify the entity.

It was Buddy Wilson, one of the murder victims. I sensed his presence in the car with me. I kept telling myself that it wasn't happening.

Bill, please keep an eye on my wife Lauren for me. She's going to need your support and friendship. Let her know that I'm fine and will remain close to her. My family will also need your help. Thanks for being here for us.

It didn't make any sense. I'd never even met him. Why pick me? How could he trust me like that? I was in shock and didn't respond. Although there was no other communication, I felt his energy for the remainder of the commute. His spirit was warm and loving. I wanted to tell him—'I'm really sorry this happened to you.' I'm sure he already knew what I was feeling. Our bond was comforting and, at the same time, spooky.

As I walked into M1, Terri approached me.

"Bill, we've just assigned Human Resources managers for each family. You'll be assisting me in overseeing the entire process and working with Laura Black's family."

"But who's been assigned to Buddy Wilson's family?" I asked.

"Desiree," she replied.

"Terri, I think I'd like to work with the Wilson family."

"Are you sure? I'd really like you to handle the Black family."

"No problem..I'll do that as well."

"Hmm, why don't you check with Desiree and feel her out on it. I don't want her to think we're not confident of her abilities."

Walking up to Desiree, who was also fairly new to the company and about my age, I knew in all likelihood that she wouldn't be open to giving up her assignment. Buddy was part of the Information Systems group which Desiree regularly assists, and she had worked relentlessly to establish her credibility with them. Although hesitant, I could feel Buddy's energy, egging me on. *Go...Bill...Go!*

"Morning, Desiree...how are you doing?" I asked.

"Okay, I guess," she responded.

"Desiree...would you mind if I assisted you with the Buddy Wilson family?"

The expression on her face indicated uneasiness. Initially her big brown eyes popped open and it appeared she was mouthing the word, 'No.' But something happened. She became calm, and what came out of her mouth may have even surprised herself.

"Bill, I think that would be a great idea," she replied.

As I walked out of the conference room, Bob Kohler's secretary Kathy motioned to me.

"Bill, someone named Harry Bowlin has been in the lobby waiting for you. I told him you were extremely busy today, but he insisted on seeing you."

"Alright, thanks Kathy."

As soon I stepped out into the lobby, Harry jumped from his seat and rushed toward me.

"Bill, I was so worried about you. I kept calling last night but they wouldn't put me through to you. I didn't sleep a wink. I can't believe you went back in the building."

"Thanks for your concern, Harry—I'm okay. We're just busy dealing with everything," I said.

"Bill, I feel so bad. That Farley guy was right in front of me. When I arrived in the parking lot, he was across from me in the motor home. He was staring at me. I could have been killed as well. He must have been waiting for me to leave before he got out and entered the building."

"Harry, have you told the police about this? They need to have this information."

"Yes, I gave my statement to them yesterday."

"Good," I said.

I excused myself, informing Harry that his interview would be rescheduled when things settled down.

Looking out from the lobby, I saw that cameras and reporters were still hovering around. They appeared to be disrupting traffic. I alerted the guard sitting at the reception desk to this. The media folks were circling around like vultures.

The company had already issued a "gag order" for employees. Supervisors relayed messages to the wounded at home and in hospitals not to discuss the incident. Management had thought ahead—they wanted Farley prosecuted locally. A change of venue was not acceptable. Whispers of death penalty were already echoing off the walls of every ESL building.

In the early afternoon, one of the victims' brothers arrived to pick up their vehicle. He needed help locating the keys. I was asked to go over to M5 and search the murdered employee's office. I asked that a security representative accompany me to verify the procedure.

We entered M5 through the south entrance and walked through the area of my department. The lights were off and not a sound was heard. For some reason, it felt more deserted than nights I worked there alone.

The large window between our offices and the lobby was shattered by gunfire. Pausing in front of my door, I noticed damage to the carpeting. *Damn*, I thought. *Farley came gunning for us in Human Resources to retaliate for his firing.*

The bullet that shattered the window ricocheted where I normally stood. I would have been shot through the heart. Looking up, I visualized Farley standing at the top of the stairs firing at me. I almost screamed.

I felt uneasy as soon as we stepped into the dead employee's office on the second floor. Piles of paper were scattered on top of his desk; an attaché case sat upright on the floor; a brown sports jacket hung loosely on a hook. As I placed my hands in the jacket pockets, shivers ran down my spine. It was an intrusive feeling, like I was actually searching him. A torn ticket stub was found, but no keys. The center drawer of his desk was pulled out. It displayed some clutter but not what we were after. I lifted his attaché case, placed it on top of the desk and released the latches. Next to a few pieces of wrapped chewing gum was a set of keys. As we left, I silently apologized to the employee for the search.

By Thursday afternoon, some of us were allowed back into our offices to resume work. I closed the drapes in my office window that faced the parking lot. Anything to diminish feeling like a sitting duck. My desk calendar still read Tuesday, February 16, and Harry Bowlin's name in the three p.m. slot jumped out at me. For a moment, I thought it was Tuesday all over again. That gave me goose bumps.

Buddy Wilson's wife Lauren and I met in my office. It was our first face-to-face encounter. She appeared younger than twenty-one, had long blonde hair, and was dressed in jeans and tennis shoes. Although her voice was soft, she spoke clearly and succinctly. Lauren emanated strong, inner strength.

I mentioned that tours were being conducted of the crime scene for employees and families wishing to spend time in the area for therapeutic purposes.

"Do you have any desire to participate?" I asked.

Suddenly she sat up, leaned forward, and said, "Actually, Bill, I want to go into Buddy's office...where he died."

I was shocked. Her request was not unusual, but still it caught me off-guard. "Well, let me look into that," I replied.

"Let me know as soon as you can. I'm meeting with the benefits department tomorrow morning and would like to go in at that time. I'd also like to be alone," she said.

"I'll call you as soon as I know something," I replied.

It was perhaps an overreaction, but I was concerned that she may be despondent and harm herself where Buddy died.

I walked her out and notified Terri, who spoke immediately with Lew and Bob. They understood my concerns. Farley killed Buddy with a shotgun blast to the head and his office was a gory scene.

Her request was honored—a requisition was approved for crews to work through the night. Furniture and equipment had to be moved out. Carpeting needed replacing; walls had to be repaired and painted.

The conversation Lauren and I had on the telephone that evening was enlightening. It started off somewhat formal.

"Lauren, workers are going to be making repairs this evening. When you come in, we'd like to have you meet with Charlene, who is a grief counselor. After that, assuming the office is ready, we'll bring you over there. If not, we'll have you meet with the benefits folks first. Charlene will be arriving at nine a.m. How does that sound?"

"Thanks for all your help, Bill. I think I met Charlene—there were just so many people I spoke with today."

"I hope everyone is being helpful. I can't begin to imagine how difficult this must be for you," I said. "Somehow, I know the love you and Buddy shared was very special, and just because he's not physically here any longer, his spirit will always be with you."

"Bill, if you knew me before this, you'd be surprised at how I'm holding up. There is no way I'd have the strength. But Buddy *is* still with me. I can feel him! He's keeping me together...helping me get by."

"So you *do* sense Buddy around at times?" I inquired.

"Oh yes!...yes!"

"Lauren, are there times that his presence is stronger? Or certain places?"

"You know, we bought a new car recently, and I feel Buddy in the car when I'm driving....and in our apartment. He talks to me. He's spoken to you also, hasn't he?"

"What?!" I replied.

"C'mon, Bill, I can tell by how you're talking to me," she implied.

"Yeah, you're right," I said. "I *have* felt his spirit...it began Wednesday morning. I was surprised because he and I had never met."

"It doesn't matter. I know he trusts you, Bill—as I do," she said.

We were on the phone for hours, becoming fast friends and kindred souls—Lauren, myself, as well as Buddy. Just knowing that my friendship could help ease their pain in some way made my grueling six months at ESL worth it. I felt honored to serve as a medium for Buddy.

That Friday morning, the north section of M5's first floor was closed off for Lauren. She called my office around ten a.m.

"Bill, Charlene and I are coming over now. Should we meet you by Buddy's office?"

"No—why don't you come over to my office and we'll go from here," I said.

As soon as we hung up, I darted out of the office to check with the facilities people on the repairs. Steven Donovan, the Security Manager, was stepping out of Buddy's office as the foreman approached.

"How's everything going?" I asked.

"They just got done moving everything back in," Steve replied. "I double-checked to make sure no traces were left that may upset her. Is she here?"

"Yeah, she's on her way," I said. "Now, the other folks aren't coming in until we're done, right?"

"Absolutely," Steve replied. "My people are keeping this side of the building off-limits until you give me the word."

"Perfect," I said.

"So, whenever you're ready, Bill," Steve said.

"If you don't mind, I'd like to go in and check the office as well," I said.

"I think everything's okay, but suit yourself," he said.

As I entered the office, the foreman followed me in.

"There's something you should know," he whispered.

"What's that?" I asked.

"You see, we moved the desks and equipment out last night. There was other furniture out here. So this morning when we finished, we rushed to get everything back in. I'm sorry, but the desk that's in there doesn't belong to the victim who was inside. It's from another office," he said.

"Alright, but there's nothing we can do about that now," I replied.

I sat down at the desk. I conducted a thorough inspection of the room. Drawers were virtually empty. Nothing else was on the computer or desk. Anything sharp such as scissors or a letter opener were sought for removal; loose cords as well. Satisfied, I returned to my office, where Lauren and Charlene were waiting.

"How are you this morning, Lauren?" I asked.

"I'm alright," she answered, with a courteous smile. "Can we go over now?"

Charlene then stepped up between us, placing a hand on each of our shoulders.

"Let me tell Bill what we talked about. Lauren's going in the office by herself. We agreed that after twenty minutes, if she hasn't come out, I will check on her. Is that correct?" Charlene asked, looking directly at Lauren.

Lauren nodded.

Charlene, Steve Donovan, and I stood inside the north entrance as Lauren walked alone down the corridor. Her movements were slow and delicate. She wore a crew neck tee-shirt tucked into her jeans and tennis shoes; no jacket or purse. She stopped in front of his office, turned and walked in, closing the door behind her.

The rest of us stood and engaged in small talk. Periodically, I leaned away from the group and listened for sounds from the room...none. I glanced at my watch obsessively, but it brought no relief. As each minute passed, I was becoming a nervous wreck.

At ten-forty a.m., twenty minutes after Lauren entered, Charlene strolled past and said, "I'm going to see how she's doing." She walked softly down the hall, knocked twice, paused, and went in. Steve and I just looked at each other and shrugged.

Shortly thereafter, Lauren and Charlene stepped out. Charlene had her arm around Lauren, who was holding something against her chest. As they reached us, Lauren stepped toward me.

"Please Bill, I have to have this!" she cried.

"What is it, Lauren?" I asked.

"This is Buddy's notebook. There's nothing in there that's confidential. He kept this as a journal and made notes about his work, his boss, and the friends he had here. Please, Bill, it's important to me!"

"Let me take a quick look, Lauren," I said.

As she reluctantly passed it to me, I held the booklet gently, to preserve its spiritual energy. It was your standard engineering notebook that each department issued. The cover was blue; lines were "college-ruled"; it was stitch-bound; and the dimensions were seven and one-quarter inches by nine and one-quarter inches.

Steve Donovan and I stepped to the side and reviewed the contents. There were a few technical notes, but most of the writings were personal. Lauren continued pleading her case. We stepped into an office and dialed a number of extensions. Unsuccessful attempts were made to reach Terri, Bob Kohler, Lew Franklin or Steve's boss.

"Steve, why don't we release the notebook to her," I suggested. "Are you comfortable making this decision with me?"

"I don't have a problem with that," he responded.

"Let's make copies of the notes for ESL records," I added.

"Good idea," he said.

We returned to Lauren, who was anxiously awaiting a decision.

"I'm going to photocopy the pages and bring the notebook right back," I said.

Walking back to my department, I passed Terri's office but she had not returned. I proceeded to the copy room. The notebook was carefully opened and copied—about fourteen pages. When it was handed back to Lauren, she clutched it like a lost puppy. "Thank you!...thank you!" she exclaimed. Company executives later reviewed the notes and supported our decision.

That evening, on the telephone, Lauren and I recapped the day's events.

"Were you okay being in the office today, Lauren?"

"Oh yeah, I was hoping to sense Buddy there—but he wasn't."

"If you don't mind me asking, what were you doing in there?"

"I was just sitting...waiting," Lauren stated.

"So where did you find the notebook?" I asked.

"It was right on top of the desk," she responded instantly.

"Whoa...really?"

"Yeah, why?" she asked.

"Lauren, I went in there right before you did and there wasn't anything on the desk. In fact, that's not even Buddy's desk."

"That doesn't surprise me. I feel Buddy's spirit in the notebook and I know he wanted me to have it. He made sure I got it."

"Amazing!" I said.

It was such a powerful, spiritual sign. We didn't have the answers to why such a horrific event took place, yet, amidst the sorrow and pain, hope and love loomed. The guy above was doing his best to help us through this. Perhaps he also wanted me to believe in him again.

A memorial service for all the victims was held Thursday, February 25, at two p.m., nine days after the massacre. Dark clouds loomed above as the somber event began. In the south parking lot of M5, folding chairs had been meticulously laid out across the pavement and a giant platform erected. We expected two thousand people; it was standing room only as many more showed up. Television cameras were lined along the perimeter.

Red and white carnations were worn by family members, speakers, guests and other participants. The flowers also identified invitees of a special reception following the service.

During the service, I served as host to Buddy's and Laura Black's families. Debbie Norton, Buddy's mother, arrived from Southern California. Although we had spoken daily by telephone, the face-to-face meeting was an experience I will never forget.

A large group of us were inside M5 preparing to walk out to our seats. As Desiree was pinning a carnation on me, an attractive blonde woman made her way through the crowd and approached me. She suddenly wrapped her arms around my neck and proceeded to give me a big hug.

"Oh, Bill, it's so good to meet you," she said.

Her voice confirmed her identity.

"Debbie?" I asked.

"Yes, of course," she responded.

"But how did you know who I was?" I asked. (I wasn't the only Asian male in the area.) "Did someone point me out to you?"

"No, not at all," she replied. "I walked in, saw you and just knew."

"That's incredible," I said.

Debbie then stepped aside and nudged a shy teenage boy forward. I didn't notice anyone behind her. The next words she spoke caused my mouth to drop.

"Bill, I'd like you to meet Buddy's brother...Eric."

My heart stopped. *ERIC?!...ERIC?!*

(My son's full name is Eric Wilson Lee. I nicknamed him "Buddy" when he was about three. At first, I accepted Buddy Wilson's name as a mere coincidence. But when the name Eric was mentioned, it was undeniably a powerful spiritual message. It confirmed my fate at ESL.)

After regaining my composure, I debated whether to say anything, but the words just spilled out.

"Debbie, my son's name is also Eric; his middle name is Wilson; and his nickname is Buddy!"

My comment didn't seem to faze her. She calmly replied, "Bill, there's no doubt in my mind that you were meant to be in our lives. You've helped us tremendously. I know you're here at ESL for a reason. I sensed it when we first spoke on the telephone."

She was absolutely right. I didn't need any more proof.

When the service concluded, clouds directly overhead opened up and the sun broke through, as if the souls of our beloved co-workers were rising to heaven.

As mourners slowly made their way out, our seating section retreated to M5. Approximately two hundred of us gathered inside for the reception. In addition to family members and co-workers, many of those involved in the crisis were present, including counselors and police personnel.

Feeling a tap on my shoulder, I turned and saw Lieutenant John Griffin. I had not seen him since the siege. As we shook hands and engaged in small talk, an employee stopped and praised us. "You two did a great job that day," he said. John smiled and I went along. It was a facade; I was actually feeling queasy. Standing with the lieutenant brought me back to the command center. Images suddenly flashed of family members crying and police SWAT team members running. I immediately blocked them out, using the same skills I developed early in life.

On March 9, I walked into Terri's office and turned in my resignation. She knew there wasn't any room for discussion. We had come to terms on my role there.

"You know, Terri, I've never felt right in the job. During our interviews, I knew coming here wasn't about the work. Yet something told me I needed to be here. I didn't know what it was until the crisis occurred."

"Bill, I understand what you're saying and agree. I know you've often questioned your decision about accepting the job. Then again, I don't know how we would have dealt with the massacre without your help. You really made a difference."

I personally notified Lauren, Buddy's mother Debbie Norton, and Laura Black of my impending departure from ESL. Most of the issues I was assisting them with had been resolved.

All of us indicated we wanted to stay in touch, but none of us did. That didn't surprise me. Sometimes you meet people in passing and still have a powerful impact on one another.

The last conversation Lauren and I had by telephone illustrated this. It occurred just days before I left the company.

"How are you doing?" I asked.

"I'm alright, I guess," she said. "It's just that..." (long pause).

"Lauren, what were you going to say?"

"Bill, I need to ask you something...have you sensed Buddy at all the past few days?"

"Hmm...actually, I haven't. But that doesn't surprise me. Why do you ask?

"When Buddy first died, I felt him around a lot. But it's become less frequent. Lately, I don't sense him at all," she said sadly. "Bill, did you just say you aren't surprised?"

"Yes," I replied.

"Why?" she asked.

"Well, in my culture, we believe that spirits of the deceased may return to visit people close to them following their death...before they move on."

"Wow," she reacted. "Have you ever experienced it—before Buddy?"

"Yes, it's happened several times," I replied. "It scared me at first."

"So do you think...Buddy's moved on?" she asked nervously.

"Lauren, this is just my opinion. I believe Buddy will always be with you. I think there are various phases that spirits go through. Initially, they may be around us, but eventually, they move on—to a spiritual realm such as heaven. That's why it's important for us to let go. That doesn't mean we forget about them or disregard their existence. In fact, they're probably watching over us but we may not be aware of it. Does that make sense?"

"Yes, it does. Is that why you're leaving ESL?" she asked.

"Sort of. My work's done here...it's time for me to return to my consulting practice. I need to move on. And my clients are pressuring me," I said half-jokingly.

"Can I call you from time to time?" she asked.

"Of course you can," I replied.

Lauren and I never spoke again. I called several times, leaving messages, but didn't get a response. The fact that we met under such difficult circumstances may have something to do with it. Perhaps the people she met as a result of Buddy's tragic death reminded Lauren of that horrible event in her life; a period she needed to move on from.

After leaving Electromagnetic Systems Laboratories, I returned to my consulting practice, convinced that I had fulfilled my spiritual mission there. I accepted all the trauma in my life—from my home and the streets, as well as my experience in counseling, as prerequisite training for my assignment at ESL. This could have been a nice ending to the story.

Unfortunately, I was still entrenched on the dark side, continuing to lie, cheat and hustle, in all areas of my life. I convinced myself that my role during the ESL crisis made up for all the bad deeds I committed in the past as well as the present. I thought to myself, *God owes me "big time." If I wasn't such a punk throughout my life, I wouldn't have been able to save my co-workers.* While I was preoccupied being arrogant, I was also experiencing the worst nightmares in my life. My dark voyage was not over.

EPILOGUE

FALL, 1996

The San Francisco Police Department's Gang Task Force was formed after the 1977 Golden Dragon Massacre. Its officers had me under surveillance and they were presently tracking my runaway son. When I filed a missing person report on Eric, the GTF informed me that he had been recruited into Chinatown's most ruthless gang.

It was after three a.m. on a cold, foggy morning, as my car crawled through Waverly Alley and came to a stop at the entrance to Chinese Playground. Haunted by the violence and other horrifying experiences that took place here, I swore nearly twenty years ago never to return.

The sidewalk was deserted as I walked in the main level, which was pitch dark. Scowling in frustration at the burned-out bulb atop the street light, I prayed to find Eric, unharmed and willing to return home with me. I had not seen or heard from him in weeks. Officers of the Gang Task Force who were closely monitoring gang activity in Chinatown, reported that an "Eric Lee," age fourteen, was questioned there earlier in the evening when a major fight broke out. That unnerved me. Rival gangs, including those I fought against in the 1970s were still clashing over the playground to claim it as their turf. As I combed the grounds, which bore no resemblance to my childhood sanctuary, there wasn't a single soul in sight.

Returning to my car, I sat and reflected on my upbringing of Eric, wondering what I did wrong. Perhaps being more open about my past might have deterred Eric from the gangs. He also sensed something dark about his grandfather, which I concealed from him.

When my father passed away in 1992, we held one of the most lavish Chinese funerals in the city's history. Eric, who was only ten, was curious about a particular group of men who participated in the final rites. They were the top elders of Chinatown's most powerful Tongs. As each took their turn and bowed in front of the casket, a Cantonese-speaking woman sitting behind us made a comment.

"Dad, what did she say?" Eric asked.

"It was nothing," I replied.

Her comment was that she had never seen all the "dragon heads" or underworld leaders together in one place. I didn't see any purpose in tainting Eric's perception of his grandfather or his associates. I wanted Eric to have positive role models and to keep him as far away from the underworld as possible.

My next stop was a video arcade on the Broadway strip, where three Asian youths, Eric's approximate age, were hovering around a loud, flickering machine, cussing in both Cantonese and English. Lit cigarettes dangled from the sides of their mouths. Two of them turned quickly and gave me the once-over. The third one, with streaks of dyed blond hair, was gripping the zippered edge of his black jacket with his elbow tucked in—a conspicuous sign that he was packing. Whether or not they knew the whereabouts of my son, I had to restrain myself from attacking them out of frustration. Deep down, I'd never been so scared in my life.

My fear was that Eric was following in my footsteps and would experience similar horrors on the streets. I knew all too well how the *dai los* or gang bosses exploited fresh recruits. I was in a state of panic. All the trauma in my life combined didn't equate to the anguish

I felt knowing that my family's dark legacy had been passed down. My father couldn't keep me out of the Hock Sair Woey, and now I faced the same predicament with my son.

Desperately seeking out my long-time psychotherapist Ellen, who had always been there for me, I discovered that she was no longer available. Ellen, who was only in her forties, had passed away unexpectedly. The difficulties with my son and the loss of Ellen unleashed all my past demons, from Chinatown to Silicon Valley. I felt hopeless and alone, suspecting God of using me just so he could save others. And now he was abandoning me in my greatest time of need. I was emotionally bankrupt. That's when I hit rock bottom.

The crisis I went through was a humbling experience which forced me to examine and transform my life. I realize now that returning to Chinese Playground was essential for me to let go of my past and move away from the dark side. This is where it all began—my obsession with winning, bullying people, making money and being a good soldier. The playground is where I sought refuge and learned to numb my early childhood pain of feeling unwanted and worthless. My parents' crude attempt to abort my birth and to sell me away was simply the start of my problems.

Beginning as a young boy, my engagement in high-risk and self-destructive behavior served as a powerful narcotic for me and I became addicted to the action. When I jumped across rooftops, gambled, fought, dodged bullets or won a corporate battle, the euphoria offered a temporary reprieve from my suffering. My view of the world was bleak. But the more I lied, resorted to violence, stole, cheated, and hustled, the worse I felt about myself.

Sadly, the reason why I was able to stay calm and assist others in crisis situations is due to the fact that I was constantly on edge. I didn't feel safe—anywhere or anytime. Life—in my view, was one giant minefield. I survived by tiptoeing around, being cautious and suppressing my emotions, especially fear.

God has guided me on an amazing journey. On numerous occasions, he chose me to save others. God never abandoned me. He brought me back to Chinese Playground for my most important mission—to save myself.

My initial objective in writing *Chinese Playground* was to draw attention to the dark side of the Chinese culture. As my life has been transformed and my soul is healing, I hope this story touches and provides encouragement to people of all cultures struggling with their own childhood demons. The world is a terrifying place for a child who doesn't feel safe or loved. Unfortunately, there are too many people out there seeking refuge in their own dark world. They cope with their pain by obsessing in food, diet, alcohol, narcotics, gambling, shopping, sex, self-mutilation, cosmetic surgery, violence, competition, work, and the list goes on and on. But if I can learn to trust and find decency in myself, others can as well. The tendency is to try to do it alone, but the miracle of recovery fellowships is the love and support that is bountiful. The vulnerable child in all of us deserves to be loved and cared for.

I am presently on hiatus from the high-tech industry and continue to work hard on my recovery. I am committed to serving as a good role model for Eric, who is entering college.